Handbook
of
Discovery Techniques
in
Elementary School Teaching

Also by the Authors:
Personalized Behavioral Modification:
Practical Techniques for Elementary School Teachers,
1976, Parker

Handbook
of
Discovery Techniques
in
Elementary School Teaching

P. Susan Mamchak
and
Steven R. Mamchak

Parker Publishing Co., Inc.   West Nyack, N.Y.

Library of Congress Cataloging in Publication Data

Mamchak, P   Susan,
  Handbook of discovery techniques in elementary school
teaching.

  Includes index.
  1. Learning by discovery. 2. Motivation in education.
I. Mamchak, Steven R., joint author. II. Title.
LB1065.M32   372.1'3   76-56360
ISBN 0-13-377234-9

Printed in the United States of America

Dedication

. . . to the memory of Steven Mamchak, Sr.,
who continues to live in the hearts of those
who loved him.

How This book Will Help You, The Professional Educator

Ever mindful of the Henry Adams observation that, "A teacher affects eternity; he can never tell where his influence stops," teachers have always realized that what is done today may have its implications days, months, or even years later in the child's life. Is it any wonder, therefore, that we constantly seek new and effective ways to help our students "discover" the vital, fascinating ways education can affect their lives?

Especially in the elementary classroom, we need programs and specific activities that will help us make learning exciting and enticing. Yes, *enticing,* for we have always known that if a child wants to learn something, he will learn it. If he can be taken to the point where *he* is seeking an answer, he will find it. And if, along with this search, he can be guided to find the answers, only to become aware of more questions beyond the place where he has come, and is motivated to follow that path to its destination, then education has, indeed, taken place.

The difficulty has always been to achieve this goal in the day-to-day operation of our classrooms where we are faced with such diverse problems as:

***Utilizing the physical setup of the classroom in order to achieve its potential as a center of learning . . .
***The negative outside influences that prejudice students . . .
***The gifted child who becomes bored and seemingly "turned off" to school . . .
***The behavior problem who robs himself and his classmates of valuable learning time . . .
***The underachiever who frustrates our every attempt to help him . . .

The list goes on and on, and at times it seems an insurmountable problem.

Yet there are ways, despite these obstacles, in which you *can* lead your students to discover their full potentials as learners and as developing human beings—practical, tested methods which have worked with a broad range of problems in real-life situations and under a variety of conditions.

The term we will be using for these methods of success is "Discovery Technique." "Discovery Technique" is a generic term for a teaching method that meets certain criteria. It must:

1. Engender interest, and/or
2. Increase academic achievement, and/or
3. Develop skill and conceptual growth on the part of the student.

In short, a Discovery Technique is a carefully structured method that "turns on" a kid to learning and motivates him to learn more. For example . . . .

***Alice, with her 153 IQ, was a real problem. Bored by her fifth-grade work, she wasted time and alternately mocked or taunted her classmates beyond their endurance. Her teacher, however, initiated a series of tasks for Alice that of their very nature engendered discovery. For example, when asked to write a comparison piece on Easter and Passover for the class newspaper, Alice discovered that there were many similarities. With careful guidance by her teacher, Alice was soon engrossed in the study of Middle East geography, history, and politics. Very soon Alice found that she had too much to learn to waste her time, as answer led to question and she discovered the challenge and the joy of learning.

***All Tommy wanted to be was a spaceman. He day-dreamed constantly; his English was poor, and his math was worse. Then his teacher decided to apply a discovery technique known as "The Side-Board Tactic." Tommy got to be a spaceman, all right, and discovered that his English improved (you have to keep a log on a space ship), and his math skills soared (he had to know how to convert his allowance into Martian money).

***Billy had no friends. The children feared his bullying tactics, and in class he was a constant source of distraction. Using a method known as "The Actor," his teacher showed him how to get other people to do what he wanted by making them like him. Billy never realized that in changing other people's opinions he was modifying his own behavior and personal outlook—not, that is, until he gradually discovered that he had friends, and that now, school was fun.

***"I want each of you to take a block out of the middle of this tower," the teacher said. The hands of the two children reached out, and the tower dissolved into a tangled heap on the table. "You see," the teacher continued, "these blocks are different sizes, shapes, and colors, but together they make something strong and beautiful. Take one away, and all we have left is a mess." The young black boy and the young white boy looked first at the teacher, then at the fallen blocks, and then at each other. They were beginning to understand.

These examples are representative of results that have

actually been achieved by real teachers in real classrooms by the practical application of discovery techniques in the learning process. By following the procedures outlined in this book, you will find that:

> ***Your students will begin learning because *they want to* . . .
> ***Those personality problems that so mar the progress of some students will begin to disappear . . .
> ***The quality and productivity of homework will increase . . .
> ***Your students will begin to seek out new avenues of education and begin learning how to work on their own . . .
> ***Your classroom will become that vital center of learning you always knew it could be . . .

And these are realities that are within your grasp.

This is a handbook of techniques that will help you *now*, right now, in your classroom and with your students. These discovery techniques are simple, dynamic, practical, and, most importantly of all, they *work!* Here you will find real solutions to real problems; solutions that you will use time and again and from day to day. And the only equipment needed is that one invaluable, irreplaceable tool of American education—you, the creative, sensitive teacher with the firm conviction that each child is entitled to live up to his full potential as a human being of worth and dignity. It is within your power to start your students on the path to *discovery*—discovery that learning is a joyous, ongoing process that will enrich their lives today and throughout all their tomorrows. If you firmly desire to give your students that precious gift, then we invite you to read on—and discover . . .

P. Susan Mamchak

Steven R. Mamchak

Acknowledgement

One of the delightful aspects of writing a book is that you get to meet many fine people. This book is no exception. During its planning and writing we had the opportunity of meeting and speaking with many exceptional educators. Wherever possible, we have mentioned the names of these teachers in connection with particular methods and techniques which they have graciously been willing to share with us and our readers. Along with our deep respect goes our heartfelt thanks to them not only for their contributions, but for their many courtesies and considerations as well.

For their aid, time, and consideration in helping us compile our research, we wish to thank the following: Raymond Mantley and the faculty and staff of Lenna W. Conrow Elementary School; Joseph Persiponko and the faculty and staff of Monmouth Beach Elementary School; Thomas Williams and the faculty and staff of River Street School; Joyce A. Clark and the faculty and staff of Middle Road Elementary School; faculty and staff of the Independent Study Program of Beck Middle School; Katherine Olshaker of Broad Street Elementary School; Dr. Joan Abrams, Superintendent of Schools, Red Bank; Katy Wells; Shirley Johnson; Julia Dodd; Jane Short; and Sandra Kelly of WEEI Radio, CBS-Boston.

To Mildred Mamchak and Donald Pease we offer our thanks for their encouragement and for being our parents. Also, to all the teachers and students who played a part in this book, thanks for making it such a tremendously enriching experience.

P. Susan Mamchak

Steven R. Mamchak

CONTENTS

13

Chapter 1

How to Prepare Your Class
for Discovery Techniques—
An Overview

Remember the first time you discovered something on your very own? You were probably very young, and the discovery might have been anything from the fact that boys were different from girls to the fascinating observation that flies could walk upside down, but *you* made the discovery, and *that* made it special. What pride it engendered; and what new avenues it opened for you. Suddenly you found that there was *so* much to learn, and, if you were fortunate, what you learned led only to more questions. A pattern, a hunger, a zest for learning began to form within you.

Wouldn't it be wonderful if we, as teachers, could instill that same sense of wonder in our students? If we could lead them to that point of "discovery" where they began to learn because they *wanted to learn,* what a gift we would give! Why not? If we can conceive of the idea, then there must be ways to make it a reality. Perhaps the first step is to look at our classes and determine the precise goals we wish them to accomplish.

DETERMINING THE GOALS
FOR YOUR CLASS

Let's take a look at *your* classroom. You are the one who knows it best, for it is the place where you spend a large part of your life. Picture it in your mind as we ask a few questions.

First, how many students do you have? This is important, since the goals for a class of 18 will, of necessity, differ from those for a class of 35 or 40. The physical limitations of size must be considered in determining goals, for a goal that is impossible to attain becomes a frustrating liability rather than a functioning asset.

Next, what is the age and sexual makeup of your class? Remember, to set goals which aim at successful interaction between boys and girls and require them to work closely together may be laudable, but depending on the age of your class, you may be creating your own problems. Certainly we've all heard the statement, "I ain't gonna work with no girl!" followed by an equally firm, "Boys are icky!" Wouldn't it be better to allow them to discover that they need each other, rather than set goals which require compulsory companionship?

Now, this may seem irrelevant, but what can your class see from the windows of your room? Given an elementary school classroom that faces a fire station, there is nothing you can do to keep attention once those trucks start to roll! A classroom that faces, conversely, on an idyllic pasture scene becomes a springtime daydreamer's paradise. As teachers, we are well aware of the myriad distractions that steal learning time from students and frustrate our efforts to teach. Let us be equally aware of them when we begin to set the goals for our class. That fire house, for instance, might become a lesson in civics, with each student timing the seconds between bells and the time the first truck leaves. Sure, it still interrupts the lesson, but instead of wasting time, now the children are involved and learning.

And finally, what subject are you teaching? Are your classes departmentalized or do you teach the majority of your class's subjects? If you teach only English, you had better be certain that the math and history teachers concur before you go planning any interdisciplinary approaches. Your idea of any given goal may differ drastically from another teacher's view of it. Moreover, if your classes stay with you all day, the situation may call for a different type of rapport than comes from a situation where you see them for 45 minutes only.

Putting all these answers together, what have we discovered

about determining goals for our classes? Perhaps we can summarize this way:

>When setting goals for our class, let's make certain they are:
>1. ATTAINABLE—something that has the best chance of working for the most students.
>2. REALISTIC—within the physical limitations of our room and our student's abilities.
>3. COMPREHENSIVE—incorporating everything we know about our room, our students, and our school.

Keeping these in mind, we will have set goals for our class with which they can work, and discover, and grow.

WHAT IS YOUR CLASS LEARNING?

Now that we have determined where we want to go, let's take a look at where we are. Let's see what our classes have learned, are learning, and what they need to learn.

What is "learning?" Philosophers have pondered the question, psychologists have researched it, everyone is concerned about it, but what is it? Perhaps the question will never be fully answered, but certainly we can tell you what it isn't. It isn't the parrotting back of material. To have a child memorize a list of dates and then repeat them back to you may show his capacity for memorization, but it does not prove that he has learned a thing. Learning involves internalization, the ability to take in facts and then *apply and use those facts* in day-to-day life. To memorize a line of poetry is fine, but to take that same line, apply it to your own life and find within it wisdom and joy and solace—that's learning!

Nor are we convinced that the volume of input has anything to do with learning as a viable, dynamic process. We have met teachers who have literally deluged classes with facts. Those facts were subsequently returned to the teacher by dutiful students. We are certain the material passed, but we're not too sure how much learning took place. Conversely, there are teachers of our acquaintance who have concentrated on quality far more than quantity. These teachers have the remarkable and invaluable ability to get to the heart of the matter, to present material to their students which fires them with curiosity, with insatiable yearning for more, with determination to find out. By the end of the year, their kids are applying what they have learned. They are doing homework and class exercises as a means to an end, and *not* as an end in itself. They have learned.

In terms of your own class, ask yourself how much of last year's learning they can use? For that matter, how much do they use of last month's learning? Last week's? Yesterday's? There are some ways in which we can find out:

TESTING—We can always test to find out where our students are. Just be careful it's not a case of too much, too soon. A battery of tests the first week of school, even if they are diagnostic, may prove a shattering burden for some classes.

CORRELATED REVIEW—Before actually beginning a unit, we may wish to review the skills needed for it. From such an activity, a great insight into student skills may be gained.

FREE-FLOWING DISCUSSION—During discussion with our class, whether introductory or as a pastime, we may weave in such questions or subjects as will reveal their status.

THE INFORMATIVE GAME—A game, whether in the form of a spelling bee or the game of trivia, may prove a revealing tool for us while an intriguing activity for our class.

Furthermore, any of these activities may be conducted on various levels: class-wide or individually; for one or multiple subjects; for academic or social development.

Here is a technique one teacher used to test student retention of basic math skills. She called it:

QUICK AS A FLASH—The teacher divided the class into three sections. Prior to the start of the activity she had taken a set of primary grade flash cards (K-2) and a set of middle grade flash cards (3-5) and had shuffled them together to insure random order. Each group was given a team name (selected by the students), paper was passed out, and each child placed his own and his team name on it.

The teacher walked in front of the first team and displayed the first card. No reading or comment was made. The students in that team wrote down the problem and what they thought was the correct answer. After about 45 seconds, the teacher proceeded to the next team and held up the next card. This was continued until all the cards had been exhausted. The teams then exchanged papers, and the correct answers were called for (either from a specific group or a particular individual). If two more than one half the number in a particular team had the correct answer, the team was given a point which was recorded on the blackboard. At the conclusion of the activity, the team with the most points was given a prize.

This activity which took the teacher approximately 20 minutes to prepare initially, proved invaluable in allowing her to pinpoint specific areas where more work was needed while providing enjoyment for her class. Here, the emphasis was on math, but with the use of cards geared to spelling, word recognition, phonics, etc., the activity can easily be adapted to other subjects.

Once you have determined what your class has learned and is learning, you will have this information as a useful guide when determining your approach to a particular unit or subject.

CHECKLIST OF AVAILABLE MATERIAL

Now that we have set our goals and determined what is needed, what will we use to accomplish our purposes? We are speaking now of actual physical entities. Certainly we have textbooks, and paper, and pencils, and blackboard, but is that all we will use? Look at the following list:

Magazines
Bottlecaps
Egg Cartons

The Cardboard Cores from Bathroom Tissue and Towels
A Broken Doll
A Shoe Box

Can you conceive of how you might use these items to bring education to your students? One teacher taught Medieval History with them. Her class learned as they made a castle (shoe box, cardboard centers from towel rolls, parts of the egg carton) peopled by knights carrying shields (bathroom tissue cores, faces cut from magazines, bottlecaps painted silver) and ruled by a queen (the broken doll repaired). The students had a great time with it, and they learned something about history in the process. In fact, some were even inspired to do research on their own into such subjects as heraldry, costuming and architecture.

The point is, almost anything can be a learning material if we add to it the precious extra—imagination. Be innovative, and you will find no dearth of materials to be used in leading your classes toward discovery and to augment what your class is learning.

BLUEPRINT FOR AN EXPANDING CLASSROOM

Perhaps in the heading for this section we have used an inappropriate word. If all is as it should be, you will notice that your students will be the ones expanding as your classroom begins to shrink!

Let us explain. Do you remember your concept of the world when you were a child? At first, the world consisted of your room, the rest of your home, and perhaps the back yard. Later, as you grew, the world became an area, three or four blocks perhaps, with your home still at the center. Still later, when you entered school, your world expanded to include that as well. In college, the world expanded still further, until now, as an adult, with the full impact of media and mobility, *the* world is truly *your* world. Your room at home may still be there, the same one which, as a child, seemed so vast and which your imagination changed with a hundred fulfilling visions, but when you return the toys are packed away on the shelves and the room itself seems so small . . . so small.

Not that this is an occasion for sadness or longing for bygone days. No, rather it is a natural, healthy outgrowth of the developmental process; one which *must* take place if we are to become rational, functioning adults in today's world.

And so should it be in your classroom. By using discovery techniques you can be aiding your students to take the "next step." You can help them to seek answers beyond the limits of the classroom.

One teacher we know conceived of a brilliant plan which she used successfully in a self-contained classroom. The motivation was superb and the student interest was fantastic. She called it:

THE JOURNEY—The teacher had gathered a great deal of material in preparation for this unit. Besides the classroom textbooks, she had for the student's use maps of the United States with each state clearly outlined; a large outline map of the Mississippi River and the Louisiana Purchase; several atlases; and many books of appropriate reading levels on that era.

She introduced the unit as an adventure. She read the class a story which illustrated what it was like to be living in 1803. The class was then assigned the task of imagining that they were living at that time and living at the headwaters of the Mississippi at St. Louis, Missouri. They had to take a trip down the river and arrive at the delta in New Orleans. To do this they must map their course, research the types of obstacles they might encounter, plan for provisions, investigate what languages they might need, etc. They had to keep it historically accurate (no steam engines, please) and realistically possible. The whole class might be able to travel by barge, for example, but would they be able to take all their worldly possessions with them? The culmination of the unit would be the class's successful arrival in New Orleans.

This particular technique allowed for tremendous variation. For instance, each individual member of the class may have to make the journey alone (do the research, plot the course, etc.), or it might be done in groups. Each task could be handled by a group for a whole class (one group provisioning the trip, another checking on the people they are likely to meet, etc.). The class could stop and explore each area as they pass through it, and arrive at New Orleans at a future date. (This method allows for a great deal of flexibility as a student might become interested in the Indians of an area and you might let him "live" with them for a while before he "rejoins" the group.)

Whether we choose this or another method, the point is this: We can make our classroom the center, certainly, but we can expand our students' world by showing them dimensions they hadn't thought of before; help them think in other terms and lead them toward a concept of all of life as a process where the thrust is ever onward; conceive of the classroom not as a world in itself, but as the hub of an ever-changing, ever-expanding universe. This service will stand them in good stead not only in school, but in life as well.

HOW TO DETERMINE THE
SUCCESS OF PRESENT METHODS

Let's look at the techniques you are presently using. Please understand, there is no criticism either intended or implied here. By now you should have a fairly good idea of what is needed, where you are headed, and what you will use. Let's now do an honest appraisal of how you will get there.

Put quite simply, the success or failure of any given technique depends on whether or not it works! That may sound simplistic, but isn't it the truth? You may have learned an educational technique that is so brilliantly interwoven with educational psychology and so cleverly applied, that every time you use it you feel sure that your old professor of education must be smiling down on you, but if all that technique does is make you feel good while it leaves your students cold, then with all due respect to your old prof, it is not a good technique!

A good educational or learning technique is one that does precisely what you want it to do. Those are the techniques which you should sharpen and use.

That does not mean, however, that we must stop trying new

methods. We try, and sometimes we fail, but we rise to try again. That is the essence of living a successful life, and it is the mark of the creative teacher as well. Throughout this book you will find a myriad discovery techniques and be led toward making up others of your own. Try them, use them—they have all worked, time and again. Should a particular technique not work for *you,* please don't be discouraged. Discard what doesn't work and retain and cherish that which does—it is your key to success.

LISTENING FOR THE SOUNDS OF LEARNING

In classroom after classroom, we have become aware that there are five major sounds involved with education. They are:
1. Shuffling of paper and/or feet and bodies
2. Whispers and talking by students
3. The teacher's voice
4. Records, films, and other AVA equipment
5. Banging and pounding

These are constructive sounds, for they are the sounds of interaction, of the group working. Granted, they can sometimes rise to grandiose proportions, but they indicate that something positive is taking place.

There are also destructive sounds:
1. Verbal Abuse—whether from peer to peer, teacher to student, or student to teacher;
2. Pesty Sounds—a squeaky chair or the pencil sharpener when the entire class is quiet;
3. Distractions—those things we can't avoid such as knocking on the door, fire drills, and PA announcements (have you noticed that these things usually occur when you are at the high point of your lesson?).

The point of these clarifications is that in preparing our class for discovery techniques, we should make provision to keep the constructive sounds, do as much as possible to eliminate the destructive ones, and (sigh!) learn to live with the distractions, for they are as much a part of teaching as they are a part of life.

The rules we set for our class at the beginning of the year are the guidelines with which we and the children will have to live for the coming year. The rules we set should be sensible and not, of their very nature, preclude the free atmosphere in which we can listen to the constructive sounds of learning.

Here, for example, is a device which saved untold hours of classroom time in a sixth grade class. We feel it can work in your classroom as well, no matter what the grade level. It is a three step method which one teacher called:

RED LIGHT, GREEN LIGHT—Preparatory to the class's arrival in September, the teacher had made up an easily readable list of the rules of the room which she displayed prominently on the bulletin board. She had also constructed a two-sided card, one side painted red and the other painted green (actually, any two contrasting colors would do), which hung from a peg near the list of rules.

The first step was to thoroughly explain the rules of the room. She took as much time as was needed in order to insure that everyone in the class understood *why* each rule was there and *why* she demanded compliance with it.

For the second step she defined the noise levels she would and would not tolerate. She further set a numerical value to the use of constructive sounds. For example, quiet whispering was "one," while talking out loud was "two." Also, there was a key word which, she explained, was a warning about destructive sounds (This teacher used "Bozo," but any word would do.). When the class heard this word, they had gone too far and it was a demand to cease.

The third step defined the use of the two-sided card. Whenever the room was to be silent, the red side of the card was displayed. Whenever the class could have freedom of movement and speech, however, the green side would be displayed.

The value of this three step procedure became evident once the class was actually under way. Before it began she would turn the card to its appropriate side for that lesson, and signal the noise level she would tolerate ("one" or "two"). Even should some disturbances occur during class, in the majority of cases she could bring the group into compliance with a single word ("Bozo").

The value of this method is the fact that it clearly and precisely alows students to know what is expected of them. It sets clearly defined boundaries of permissible behavior and allows deviations from those boundaries to be handled with a minimum of lost time. Of course there must be a certain amount of leeway in any discipline program, but letting students know exactly what acceptable social behavior means will prove invaluable.

The sounds of learning are a symphony to be enjoyed. Use every method to squelch the destructive sounds, but let your classroom hum with learning. Everyone will benefit.

"WHEN IS A NOISE NOT A NOISE?"

We should always remember that a noise is never a noise when it is the manifestation of a mind at work. Consider this true anecdote:

It was one of those beautiful October afternoons that you save to carry you through the rain and sleet of March. The early afternoon sun slanted through the blinds on the window and covered the heads of the working students with warm golden bands. At the front of the room, I surveyed the scene. The children worked at their desks, the only sound the scratch of pencils across paper. It was a time of peace and joy, a moment to keep—quiet, still . . .

THUMP!

What was that? What was that noise?

THUMP!

There it was again! A few heads lifted, inquisitive, their gaze bouncing around the room, glancing off me, and back to their papers.

THUMP!

O.K., that's it. What fly is this walking across my painting in time? I'll put a stop to this—and quickly!

I rose from my desk and stood in the aisle between seats. My eyes scanned the room. I waited:

THUMP!

Ah, ha! There it is. That boy in the last seat is pounding his fist on the side of his desk.

"Alan," I said, "would you please step into the hallway for a moment. I want to talk to you."

"No," came the reply, "come back here. Quick, please!"

I was on my way. First disturbing the class and now insubordination. It was too much . . .

"All right, young man . . . "

"Look! Look at this!"

He pounded the desk again, and on the surface of it, his paper shook and moved a fraction of an inch.

"You see! You see!"

"Alan, what . . . "

"Remember this morning in science, when you told us about vibrations? Well, look, when I hit the desk, the paper moves. If I put my pencil up there it'll move, too. I know, I tried it out. Hey, do you think a real loud noise could make a building fall down? Huh?"

His brown eyes looked up at me filled with unanswered questions. He wasn't writing the composition assigned, but he was learning all the same. On his own he had come up with an idea, tested it out, and developed a hypothesis. He wouldn't have phrased it that way, but it is what he had done, nonetheless.

"Alan," I said as I bent down to him, "I don't know, but would you like me to tell you how to find out?"

"Yeah!"

I straightened up and looked around the room. Other faces were turned toward us.

"Class," I began, "Alan has made a really great discovery, and I'd like him to tell you about it. Alan . . . "

So far, we have determined the goals we wish to achieve with our class; we have ascertained what our class has 'learned' before, has retained, and what it needs to know; we have looked at the material we have available for our use; we have determined the philosophy and thrust of the techniques we will use;

we have examined our present options and techniques; and we have set rules which allow us to use those techniques that permit our classes to hum with the sounds of learning. In short, we have prepared ourselves and our class for the use of the discovery techniques to be found in this book.

Chapter 2

Capitalizing
on the Changing
Classroom

There is a line in a folk song of a few years ago which states, "The times, they are a-changing!" In our experience we have not met a single individual who has disagreed with that statement. Some will tell you that the change is for the better while others say it is for the worse, but certainly, the world is different today than when we were children—and it continues to change day by day. Learning to cope effectively with a changing world is a challenge which must be met if we are to function in society, and, for us as educators, an absolute necessity in view of the ever-changing nature of education and the classroom.

CHECKLIST FOR AVOIDING
STEREOTYPED TEACHING

If there is a key word in today's education, that word is "relevance." There must be relevance in what is taught, certainly, but there must be relevance in the relationship of the teacher to the class as a whole and the student as an individual as well.

We know of a teacher who, during the first weeks of her first year of teaching, asked the class to go home and bring in a magazine and a newspaper for use in the class on the following

33

day. The assignment seemed logical and easy to fulfill, and indeed, the young teacher had conceived a brilliant plan for their use. There was only one difficulty: In the vast majority of these student's homes, a newspaper was a sometime thing, and magazines were practically unheard of. Many students arrived the following day with the requested materials however, having 'appropriated' them from local newstands rather than disappoint this young, vivacious teacher with whom most of the class had fallen in love.

This incident had a happy conclusion thanks to a supportive faculty and an understanding administration, but it does seem to point out a relevant fact.

Of course every home has newspapers and magazines—in middle-class socio-economic groups, but we cannot keep the assumption when that background changes. To do so is to stereotype—to credit the characteristics of one, to all—and that is something which must be avoided at all costs if we are to teach effectively in today's society.

Does this mean that we must discard all of our personal values and mores? Of course not. Lifestyles change along with society and the backgrounds of our students, but basic values don't. Certainly we, as teachers, must and should instill honesty, truthfulness, responsibility, loyalty, and all the acceptable virtues upon which are built a happy, functioning human being. However, we must be aware of the factors which affect our class outside of school and have a direct bearing on their performance in our classroom. Also, we must become cognizant of how we, personally, may be affecting our classes.

Have you ever heard anyone:

1. Assign only boys for certain tasks (opening windows, moving books, etc.) and only girls for others (washing blackboards, dusting, etc.)?
2. Assume that a certain group or student wouldn't be interested in a particular subject?
3. Start a sentence by saying, "You understand, *they* can't be expected to . . . "?
4. Seriously comment, "Well, that nationality has a tendency toward . . . "?

All these are examples of stereotyping, and as such the attitudes they inspire can be destructive of learning and the growth of the individual. In order to avoid them, we, as teachers, must make certain that we:

1. Never make assumptions based on our own backgrounds. As in the example of the young teacher, we must be aware of how socio-economic backgrounds affect the physical necessities of the classroom;
2. Be aware of each student as an individual and treat him as such. Statements which begin, "All of them . . . " or "Every boy/girl . . . " are invariably wrong and misleading; and
3. Be ever aware of the social pressures at work within the classroom.

BLUEPRINT FOR UNDERSTANDING SOCIAL PRESSURES WITHIN YOUR CLASSROOM

It has been our experience that kids love television and spend a goodly part of their day intimately involved with it. What they see there may well influence their behavior in class as well as their relationship to their peers and adults in general.

This may seem a rather broad statement, but consider, is not the way we act socially determined by the examples of social interaction we have experienced from infancy onward? We shake hands as a social greeting, for instance, not only because someone taught us, but because we have witnessed it throughout our lives and accepted it as a folkway of our society. Had we lived in a society where people greeted each other by removing their shoes and stockings, we would be going around barefoot most of the time and considering it quite natural.

What examples of behavior do our kids experience on T.V.? Think of some prime-time shows and you will quickly realize that as far as T.V. is concerned, adults never get angry at kids, parents never spank their children, and Mommies and Daddies never yell or argue or become upset. With extremely few exceptions, parents and adults, as far as T.V. conceives of their relationship to children, are ever concerned, ever kind, ever helpful, ever smiling.

Is it any wonder, therefore, that confusion and frustration occur when life very often posits an alternate reality, one in which parents do spank, do get angry, do refuse to understand, and do argue when the money is short and the bills are long? Of course this doesn't happen in every case, all the time, but the reality of such incidents is indisputable.

Also, many young people today have a great deal going on socially outside of school. There's Boy Scouts, Girl Scouts, Little League, Pop Warner, dancing and singing lessons, etc., all with structured activities. Sometimes these activities are entered into willingly, while at other times they may have been foisted upon the child by parents or peer pressure. Norman Rockwell's painting of the piano player, baseball cap on backwards, bat and ball behind the bench, hurriedly practicing in order to join the game still holds true in many homes.

Some activities such as newspaper routes and after school jobs also eat into a child's time. Whether these responsibilities are assumed for extra pocket money or to help support the family income must be taken into consideration by the teacher. If you are wondering why the teacher should become involved with seemingly extraneous matters such as this, perhaps this personal experience will help to clarify:

I had been working with a child developing his spelling ability. On a particular day he had a great deal of trouble with a new spelling list. I had always scheduled conferences quickly, so he would not fall behind. Billy had always been prompt and, indeed, was making good progress. On this day I said I would see him after school and go over the material. Three o'clock came, and Billy did not show. I saw him the next day, and he was evasive. Rather sternly I told him to report that afternoon. "I can't," he said. "Why not?" I demanded. "I got somethin' else to do." I found myself getting angry and continued to pressure him for an answer. Finally, he blurted out through tears, "I got to work!" In a torrent of angry words he told of a family tragedy that had struck and of the part he was expected to play in the family's recovery. No amount of apology or supportive reassurance could repair the broken rapport between us.

By *knowing* the students in your class, with their pressures, their views of reality, and their responsibilities, you can aid in their growth not only in the happy times, but in the difficult ones as well.

The following discovery technique was used effectively to accomplish multiple purposes:

1. It explores group interaction.
2. It increases the student's understanding of his role within the group.
3. It allows the teacher to become aware of the various backgrounds, relevant realities, and any stereotyped thinking that exist in the class.

The technique requires only those materials that are readily available in the classroom. It is called:

MR. AVERAGE—The class was divided into workable groups. Each group was given the task of making a list of all the things which the group had in common. For example, everybody has brown hair, everybody has money in their pocket, everybody is wearing shoes, both grandparents are living, etc. Sufficient time was allowed for each group to complete the task (it was about ten minutes in the case we observed). This set of papers was collected, and the groups were then set the task of listing the differences in the group. For example, occupations of parents (as it is highly unlikely all parents would work at the same job), after school interests, jobs, ages in years and months, etc. After sufficient time had passed (again, about ten minutes), the class was brought to order. The teacher did not collect this second set of papers. On the blackboard she wrote, *Things in Common.* Under this heading she proceeded to list all those items from the first set of papers that were found in *all* groups. This completed, she made another heading on the blackboard titled, *Differences.* Now she had each group in turn read their list of differences, and she placed on the blackboard any patterns the children discovered. (Obviously, it is up to the teacher to guide the choice of patterns. If, for example, all the parental occupations were in the professions they might be listed three doctors, one lawyer, two teachers; if they were all skilled workers the list might read three carpenters, two plumbers, one mason; if the group was equally divided, it might be a four professional, three skilled, two unemployed, etc.) When all the papers were read and the blackboard lists completed, the children were given the final task of forming a picture, based on this material, of the *average* member of the class, his background, his likes and dislikes, etc. When this was completed, the teacher led a discussion, based on their results. Finally, they arrived at a common definition and the teacher wrote on the blackboard, "The average member of this class is a boy with brown hair. His father works within ten miles of this school. This boy has an after-school job, one brother and one sister, and cooks breakfast for the family on Saturday." At this point, a further discussion was begun and the individual children were asked how they fit into this picture of Mr. Average. Very quickly, the children were made to see that no *one* of them fit the picture, and that even though they might be different from that average they were nonetheless a part of it and valuable as individuals. Further, they were shown how each had contributed to the composite, and how, without them, Mr. Average would not exist.

The children in this class had learned valuable insights into individuality and the inherent dangers of stereotyping. It was a lesson they would carry with them. Each class must learn the worth of the individual, and this proved a very worthwhile and dynamic method.

HOW TO COPE WITH NEW ADDITIONS
TO THE CURRICULUM

In order for schools to remain up to date and adaptable, the curriculum is usually reviewed and changed at least once every two years. Let's look at some of these changes and mentally review how they may be affecting our classroom:

1. GIVING NEW NAMES TO OLD SUBJECTS—It is amazing how many times students can be thrown by a familiar subject given an unfamiliar title (Body Movement vs. Phys. Ed. vs. PT).

2. REORIENTATION TO SEX ROLES—Society is moving the changes in roles, duties, responsibilities, and needs into today's classroom. These changes sometimes require sensitive handling by the classroom teacher (Girls in Wood Shop and boys in Home Ec.).

3. CHANGING EMPHASIS ON VARIOUS SUBJECTS— For many reasons, subjects fall in and out of favor. Whereas last year you got all the science equipment you could use, this year you got material on American History by the carload.

4. CHANGES IN TEXT BOOKS—Students sometimes view textbooks as the logical advancement from one grade to another. He read *My Neighborhood* this year, and next year he'll read *The World Around Me*. But, if *The World Around Me* has been changed to *Inside, Outside,* may he not feel frustrated unless the change has been explained?

Another area where changes are made to improve relevance is in the teacher's policy guide. Whatever it may be called in your school, this publication explains how and under what rules you will grade, advance or retain, enter into team teaching, or change from uni-disciplinary to multi-disciplinary approaches. Even more than the changes in curriculum, a change in these guides will ultimately affect your classroom. We are not advocating that *every* change must be explained to your students, but analyze and discuss with your class any changes which might lead to misunderstanding or self-doubt.

Always remember that changing methods to suit the pressures of society requires understanding on all parts.

CHANGING ROLES AND NEW METHODS— A TEACHER'S GUIDE

We have spent some time discussing student roles that are changing, but what about the teacher? Have you ever considered the number of possible answers to the question, "What is a teacher?" Certainly, the once-prominent picture of the hickory stick, slate, and dunce cap does not fit a pants-suited, sports-minded activist of today. In fact, it is *extremely* difficult to come up with any stereotype of the modern teacher. Still, the role must be defined if an effective relationship between teacher and student is to exist.

Basically, we feel there are only three answers to our question. A teacher is either a guide or leader, an instructor or giver of information, or an enforcer and the bearer of authority. Depending on your choice of role, or combination of roles, the children will react accordingly.

Perhaps you have decided the role in which you see yourself as a teacher, but is that the one you are projecting? Would you like to find out? Take a good hold of your sense of humor and try one of these short discovery techniques, this time for teachers:

1. GUEST TEACHER—Have one of the students take over the class and see what he thinks his role is. Do this several times, and you will see the children's view of you becoming clearer and clearer.

2. DRAW ME—Have the children draw a picture of their classroom. Where they place you, what they have you doing, and even whether or not you are in the picture will give you great insight into what the children are thinking. Be sure to keep a touch of humor in mind when reviewing student drawings. After all, you know your nose can't be *that* long.

3. WHAT DO I DO?—The students are asked to decide, either in writing or orally, what a teacher does both in and out of a classroom. Besides giving you insights into how the class views you, this technique has an additional benefit because the students usually gain insight into the difficulties, similarities, and interests of people in all walks of life. Teachers really don't *live* in the school.

Once you have seen how the students view you, you may like or dislike what you find. You may have wanted to be the guide who leads them to discover the world but have stressed the rules so much that they see you as the enforcer. If you are locked into a role you don't like, there is no reason why you can't pick another and build your methods around it. You are there to educate your students; make every effort to eliminate any roadblocks to the achievement of that goal.

ROADBLOCKS TO LEARNING– SEXISM AND PREJUDICE

Two of the most destructive forces in today's classroom are sexism and prejudice. Sexism—"You can't do that because you are a boy/girl . . . "—*stops a child from learning.* The child is made to feel inferior, or rather sub-ferior (if we may coin a word), because of something over which he has no control. Prejudice—which sometimes takes the form of, "He can't be expected to do that because he is White/Black/Puerto Rican/ Jewish/Italian/Indian/French/Catholic/etc. . ."—*stops a child from reaching his full potential.* He is made to feel inferior because of *what* he is rather than *who* he is. The reasons these destructive ideas have no place in a classroom should be obvious, but exist they do, and the teacher must be ready to combat them. We must combat them in our classes and in our profession. Any teacher who is the instigator of either sexism (by role type casting of work assignments, etc.) or prejudice (personal dislike of a child because of race, creed, color, or nationality) must, justifiably, be asked to answer for it. There is no place for this type of evil anywhere, and certainly not in something we call education.

Make no mistake about it, no disconnected edict from the teacher will stop stereotyping. By constant example as well as words, we, as teachers, must *show* that we will not tolerate the attitude. Maturity, responsibility, and empathy toward one another can and should grow even in the primary grades. One boy hurling an epithet at another, be it racial or national or whatever, *isn't funny* when the boy is fourteen, and neither is it when he is five!

These two roadblocks impede not only the one stereotyped, but the one who is setting up the stereotype as well. Consequently, when dealing with discovery techniques to handle both sexism and prejudice, this two-way problem must be faced. The following two techniques have been used to break down the barriers of stereotyped thinking in the classroom. Both are very effective and, once done, leave lasting impressions. The first one is called:

> MAGAZINE MIX—The students were broken up into workable groups, and each child was given a magazine, (each *group* in the event there are not enough for all). Every time the children came across a picture of a man or woman or both doing something, wearing a uniform, playing sports, etc., it was to be cut out. The picture was then taken to the front of the room and placed in one of several shoe boxes which had been labeled *Sports, Jobs, Service,* etc. This activity was continued until each box contained at least ten pictures. The teacher then stopped the activity and regrouped the class. Each new group was given one of the boxes plus three envelopes, one marked *Male,* one *Female,* and one *Both.* Students were now asked to decide where each picture belonged and place it there. For instance, if only women could do a particular thing then the picture belonged in that envelope, if only men, then in that envelope, if both, then there. The activity was given about ten minutes. Then one person was chosen from each group to defend the groups choices for that box. The rest of the class agreed or disagreed and discussion, guided by the teacher, followed.

We have seen this technique used in kindergarten and first grade with the teacher preselecting the pictures; in a middle grade setting as part of a research project; and in eighth grade as part of a classroom debate. What is most significant is that in all cases, almost every picture will find its way into the envelope marked *Both.*

As that technique handled sexism, this next one takes on prejudice. It is direct and to the point. It was used in a first grade classroom when two boys, one black and one white, were returned from the playing field for fighting. As they entered the room they were calling each other every ethnic and prejudicial name they could think of or had heard. The teacher quickly separated them and placed them in opposite corners of the room. She then proceeded with a technique called:

> BUILD IT—Before each boy the teacher placed a set of blocks. Half the set was painted white, half black. Each boy was to build a tower with the blocks, the teacher told them, and the boy whose tower was tallest would receive a lollypop. The boys went to work and after a short time, the teacher halted the activity. She went to one boy and stood before him. "That's a very nice tower, Mark, but I forgot, you don't like black." With that the teacher reached down and removed a black block from the base of the tower and it dissolved in chaos. The procedure was now repeated with the other boy, this time using a white block. "You see," she continued, "when both white and black were together you could really build something big, and strong, and pretty. But, when you take one away, all you have is a mess." The teacher's message was so clear that both boys looked first at her and then at each other and said nothing. "Now," the teacher said, "if both of you will clean up the blocks and put them away together, you can each have a lollypop to eat on the playground."

The technique was extremely effective, and left a lasting impression. Before you dismiss it as being too simplistic, consider that prejudice is handled most effectively when you can combat it at its beginnings. Not sermons, but dramatic illustrations and personal example will be your stepping stones toward effectively dealing with the problem.

"I WANT TO BE A KINDERGARTEN TEACHER . . . GIGGLE, GIGGLE . . . "

Never have the effects of stereotyped thinking been brought home to us more effectively than in the anecdote recounted by

Dr. Bernhard W. Schneider, Superintendent of Schools in Middletown Township, New Jersey. He had been asked to speak about education as a career during a Career Day at a local elementary school. He was addressing a group of younger children when the incident happened.

"I had been talking about teaching and emphasizing the point that I was interested in seeing more men become part of the elementary school faculty, when one little boy raised his hand. I acknowledged him immediately.

" 'Can a man be a kindergarten teacher?' he asked. 'I'd sorta like to teach kindergarten.'

"Almost immediately there was outbreak of giggling in the group, fingers were pointed at the boy, and whispered conversations began. The boy who had asked the question began to blush and squirm uncomfortably. I answered quickly that of course a man could be a kindergarten teacher, and that, indeed, I was looking for just such a person, but even as I spoke it became increasingly evident to me that whatever I said, that boy had been taught a stereotyped sex role by his peers, one that would take a great deal more than my reassurance to break."

If you are interested in post scripts, Dr. Schneider found and hired a male kindergarten teacher, and together they returned to that elementary school, and spoke to that class and the boy who had asked the question. When they left, Dr. Schneider reports, the boy was beaming and the class was so impressed he was certain they had all learned a worthwhile lesson.

HOW TO THINK
IN OTHER TERMS

When we, as teachers, can learn to avoid stereotyped thinking; can learn to understand the social pressures that are at work within our classrooms; can learn to cope effectively with new additions to the curriculum; can learn to experiment and use new methods for dealing with the changing roles within our society; and can learn to combat the destructive force of sexism and prejudice, then we will indeed have learned how to think in other terms, aimed at the eradication of all barriers to the fulfillment of the child as an individual.

Rather than allowing the changing nature of today's classroom to stifle or hold us back, let us, as creative educators, learn to use it and grasp the myriad opportunities it presents to encourage discovery and wonder in our children.

Chapter 3

Determining the Direction
Your Discovery Techniques
Should Follow

Effective teaching has never been a hit or miss proposition. As a profession, we are constantly questioning ourselves not only as to how a particular method works within a classroom, but also *why* it works and whether it will work for others. Perhaps the first step is to ascertain specifically what we wish to accomplish and then set about finding those methods which will best help us attain those goals. Consequently, this chapter is geared to pinpointing where *you* want to go, what *you* want to do once you get there, and perhaps most importantly, mapping the ways in which *you* can get there again and again and again.

HOW TO JUDGE YOUR CLASS'S
"DISCOVERY POTENTIAL"

If you have been reading quietly up to this point, may we respectfully suggest that the party's over, because we're going to put you to work! Look at Figure 3-1. It is called the Discovery Potential Guide, and it is designed to help you ascertain *your* class's potential for discovery techniques. Get a fairly sturdy notebook and some looseleaf paper, and record your answers to the questions. Be sure to follow the outline and carefully number each item in your notebook. Also, leave nice large margins, as we'll need the space later. It shouldn't take you too long, and we assure you that it will be time well spent, as your answers will serve as the backbone of our further discussions of discovery techniques in your class. Everything ready? O.K., let's go!

FIGURE 3-1

DISCOVERY POTENTIAL GUIDE

Part 1–GENERAL

1. How many students in your class? How many boys? Girls?
2. What is the approximate age level of your class?
3. What subject or subjects will *you* be teaching them?
4. What subject or subjects will be taught by others? Name the other teachers with whom your class is involved. During what time slots?
5. If heterogeneously grouped, what is the approximate average
    A. Reading Level
    B. Skill Development
    C. Large and Small Motor Co-ordination
6. If homogeneously grouped,
    A. What level (A-B-C-Remedial) is your class? (Note: The terminology of homogeneous grouping may vary from school to school.)
    B. On the average, are they on/above/below grade reading level?
    C. On the average, how is their large and small motor co-ordination?
7. How do the majority of them get to school? (Walk, bus, etc.)

Part 2–ENVIRONMENTAL

1. On what floor is your classroom?
2. How close is your room to an exit/stairs?
3. Which direction does your classroom face?
4. What do the children see from the windows?
5. In relation to your room, where are
    A. Water fountains
    B. Lavatories
    C. Main offices
    D. Cafeteria, Auditorium, Gym
    E. Library

6. What kind of communication system does your school have? (Runners, telephones, PA system, etc.)
7. What noises surround your class? (Traffic? Sirens? Construction? Other?)
8. What type of outdoor recreational facilities does your school have?
9. Do students have easy access to
   A. Public Library
   B. Live Theater/Movies
   C. Magazines/Newspapers/Books
   D. Religious Centers
10. Are there any odors in the area surrounding your school? (Low tide, chemical waste, compost, etc.)
11. Are there any inherent dangers surrounding your school? (Airports, refineries, dams, etc.)

Part 3—MATERIAL

1. Is there a seat per child? Any extras?
2. Do you have a work table and chairs?
3. Does your room have
   A. Bookcase(s)
   B. Blackboards/Bulletin boards
   C. Closet space/File cabinets
   D. A Textbook/Workbook per child? Extras?
4. Does your school supply pens/paper/pencils/notebooks/ rulers/scissors/erasers? Do students supply their own?
5. Does your room have a map/globe?
6. Do you have in your room or have ready access to
   A. Record player and records
   B. Film strip/Movie projector
   C. Overhead/Opaque projector
   D. Microscopes
   E. Tape recorder
   F. Camera/VTR/Television
7. Do you order your own art supplies or is this done by the art teacher or through central supply?

Part 4—DEVELOPMENTAL

1. Do you have a class library?
2. Does your school have a student government?
3. Do you hold class elections?
4. Do you have a work list for class assignments?
5. What is your policy concerning student free time in your classroom?

6. Does your personal philosophy of discipline coincide with the rules you have established for running your room?
7. What are your disciplinary options?
8. Have you written/spoken with/personally met at least one parent/guardian per student? All? Half? Less than half? None?
9. Have you used or can you use supportive personnel? Guidance Counsellor? School Nurse? Psychologist? Disciplinarian? Supervisor?

Part 5—ACTIVITIES

1. Do you plan a class trip(s)?
2. Do you plan a class play/concert?
3. Will this activity be viewed by the entire school?
4. Will your students participate in school-wide activities? (Art shows, gym programs, science fairs, etc.)
5. Do you plan class-wide projects? If so, what kind? Written? Oral? Physically constructed?
6. Do you plan individual projects? If so, what kind? Written? Oral? Physically constructed?

That wasn't so hard, was it? If some of the questions seemed irrelevant to you, we hope you answered them anyway, as they were all carefully selected so they might capitalize on a myriad aspects of school life. As you will see later, your answers will have a direct bearing on what *you* will do in *your* classroom.

Just for the moment, however, consider the example of the young teacher and the purloined magazines which we mentioned in chapter two. Had that teacher filled out such a form, she might never have given the assignment which occasioned the incident in the first place for she would have been aware of her students' backgrounds. The form compels you to picture your classroom, school, and students *in depth*. And, as we shall see, that will prove immensely beneficial.

While we have you in the mood, we're going to ask you to complete one more assignment. Look at Figure 3-2. It is called the Personal Preference Chart. Copy this form into your notebook as well and go through the list placing a mark after

FIGURE 3-2

PERSONAL PREFERENCE CHART

SUBJECT MATTER	NOT NECESSARY	IMPORTANT	VERY IMPORTANT	ABSOLUTELY ESSENTIAL
I. LANGUAGE ARTS				
A. Teacher reading to class				
B. Students reading aloud				
C. Students reading silently				
D. Separating class into reading levels				
E. Pairing students with different reading levels				
F. Spelling, vocabulary, and composition taught together				
G. Practicing penmanship, both printed and cursive				
H. Writing letters				
II. MATHMATICS				
A. Addition and subtraction				
B. Multiplication and division				
C. Fractions, percentage, decimals				
D. Algebra and geometry				
III. SOCIAL STUDIES				
A. American history				
B. European history				
C. World history				
D. Ethnic heritages				
E. State history and geography				
F. Ideologies, concepts, philosophies				
G. Names, dates, battles				
H. Local government				
I. State and national governments				
J. Economics and consumerism				

FIGURE 3-2 (con't)

IV. NATURAL SCIENCES				
A. Students should read about subject				
B. Students should experiment with subject				
C. Students should observe experiments about the subject				
D. Students should read, write and discuss in the subject				
V. SPECIALS				
A. Teaching art concepts				
B. Teaching music appreciation				
C. Developing physical co-ordination				
D. Using cooking and sewing				
E. Teaching trade skills				
F. Media/advertising				
VI. CLASS MANAGEMENT				
Part 1 — Students **should**				
A. Raise hands before speaking				
B. Arrive in class before the bell rings				
C. Keep their desks neat and clean				
D. Act politely				
E. Keep notebooks				
F. Respect authority				
G. Do homework				
H. Line up promptly				
I. Participate in the class				
J. Use lavatory time properly				
Part 2 — Students **shouldn't**				
A. Chew gum in class				
B. Throw objects in the classroom				

FIGURE 3-2 (con't)

C. Lean back in chairs				
D. Copy work from other students				
E. Destroy property				
F. Tattle or whine				
G. Hit one another in class or playground				
H. Act up with guest or substitute in room				
Part 3 — Group Dynamics				
A. Students should work in groups of various sizes				
B. Students should work in pairs				

each item in the box which most closely approximates how vital you conceive the item to be. For example, if you think that students gain nothing by your reading aloud to them, you would check NOT NECESSARY. If, however, you think that such an activity helps improve their reading level, gives practice in concentration, etc., then perhaps you might check ABSOLUTELY ESSENTIAL.

Please remember that there are no right or wrong answers, so please check how *you really feel* about each item.

O.K., now that you have completed that task, take a black marking pen and color in the blocks you have checked.

If you turn the form on its side, so the questions are toward you, a section of which is illustrated in Figure 3-3, you will notice that it takes on the form of a graph with peaks and valleys.

FIGURE 3-3

Part 1 — Students should

	1	2	3	4
A. Raise hands before speaking		■		
B. Arrive in class before the bell rings		■		
C. Keep their desks neat and clean			■	
D. Act politely				■
E. Keep notebooks			■	
F. Respect authority				■
G. Do homework				■
H. Line up properly		■		
I. Participate in class			■	
J. Use lavatory time properly	■			

Part 2 — Students shouldn't

	1	2	3	4
A. Chew gum in class	■			
B. Throw objects in the classroom				■
C. Lean back in chairs		■		
D. Copy work from other students				■

The value of these two forms should now be becoming apparent. By glancing at the Personal Preference Chart you can see at a glance where your priorities lie. Those peaks indicate what *you* consider essential. Coupling these priorities with what you have ascertained from the Discovery Potential Guide, you will begin to see the directions that your discovery techniques should take to insure the greatest chance of success for you and your class. If, for example, you consider reading aloud to your class to be absolutely essential, but there is heavy construction going on outside your window, then perhaps shelving that priority until the road or whatever is finished would be the wisest course toward avoiding needless frustration.

Whatever the case, once you have determined where you are headed and have made note of possible pitfalls along the way, you are faced with another series of decisions—will the thrust of your discovery techniques be for an individual child, the whole class, or a combination of both?

YOUR GUIDE TO INDIVIDUAL DISCOVERY TECHNIQUES—ONE CHILD, NOT ALL

Certain techniques, of their very nature, are designed for use by individuals only. To determine if you have need of this kind of technique, ask yourself the following questions:
1. What is the problem you want to handle?
2. Is it a class-wide problem or does it affect only Johnnie or Jane?

Let's take, by way of example, something which you may have found through the correlation of our two forms. By personal preference you have decided that it is absolutely essential that your students practice penmanship. On the Discovery Potential Guide you judged that your class had excellent large motor co-ordination but average or underdeveloped small motor co-ordination. Since it is important for the development of handwriting that the child be able to manipulate his fingers, you may indeed have found something with which to work. But, that is a class problem, not an individual one. If, on the other hand, you felt that everyone had excellent large *and* small motor co-ordination except for one or two students, the problem now becomes individual.

At this point we should offer a caution—innumerable articles have been written. on techniques for individualized help for individual children, and often they are too impractical to carry out. No classroom teacher can be expected to concentrate her full effort on an individual student and expect the remainder of the class to sit like angels. In the example mentioned in the last paragraph, the individuals who need the help in penmanship should, indeed, work on it, but, *while the entire class is working on penmanship as well.* Your discovery techniques for individuals should work *within* the class structure, *not* outside of it. While it is true that one disinterested student can turn a class upside down, it is *not* conversely true that a teacher should turn a class upside down for one disinterested student.

Rather than going into various techniques and subject matters here (there will be plenty of them in later chapters on specific subjects), look at Figure 3-4 and you will see how the thrust of individual discovery techniques can be developed.

FIGURE 3-4

PROBLEM	TECHNIQUE
Poor map skills	Some students work together while most of the class works individually.
Poor phonics skills	While the class is working in the spelling workbook, some students are using the dictionary to determine the proper pronunciation of the spelling words.
Inattentiveness in class	While all students are keeping notebooks, the teacher pays particular attention to, and uses, individuals' notebooks for reference, etc.

Those mentioned in Figure 3-4 are just a few, and they will be expanded later. Just remember to keep in mind that an individual discovery technique should be looked upon as an extra shot in the arm and not radical surgery.

YOUR PLAN FOR CLASS-WIDE
DISCOVERY TECHNIQUES

What if you have discovered through the Personal Preference Guide that you would like your entire class involved in discovery? Fine, this can be handled one of three ways:
1. Group Activities
2. Entire class projects like a play or exhibition
3. An individually oriented class project

You're shaking your head over number three, aren't you? O.K., let's take that first. Probably one of the most exciting things to happen to any student or class is to find out something by accident. Teachers can use this to sponsor real joy in learning. Individuals are set to tasks which seemingly have no connection while the teacher goes on with something else. Suddenly the light dawns in first one student and then another and another and finally the whole class as they discover that their individual efforts are aimed at producing a final, connected result. When that happens, it's wild!

If you have a personal preference for projects like plays, class trips, art exhibits, etc., these can be dynamically used to spur a class to successfully discover.

Some teachers' personal preference shows their desire to involve their class in group dynamics work, the team concept of learning. This can be fantastically successful, but be sure to watch out for its pitfalls. The teacher's personality must be geared for this kind of work. There can be no traditional seating, and it does leave you with some interesting noise patterns, albeit constructive. Also, some students will have a tendency to coast if not carefully supervised.

Whatever you choose, suit it to your personality and preferences, and you will find your class-wide and individual discovery techniques tremendously rewarding. A careful combination of the two can make for even greater success.

HOW TO USE BOTH METHODS FOR THE BEST RESULTS WITHIN YOUR CLASS

So far we have shown the four separate yet interrelated parts of a successful discovery technique:
1. The Discovery Potential Guide
2. The Personal Preference Chart
3. Techniques for Individuals
4. Techniques for Classes

To these four add clear, concise rules, fair discipline, curriculum and administrative requirements, and a creative teacher possessing patience and a sense of humor, and you have the ideal discovery-oriented classroom.

The benefits to be gained and enjoyed by the students in this type of classroom are legion. Time flies, and clock watchers soon become unemployed. One task logically follows another, so day-to-day productivity keeps pace. Homework assignments are no longer disconnected from class work in the student's mind and become a real asset in understanding the working of the next day's class. One thing is certain—there is learning going on, and it is beautiful to see.

Nor is this a panacea. Of course no single discovery technique is going to accomplish this, nor will any given discovery technique be good for all classes, all subjects, or all situations, but with a well-stocked bag of them and the ability to change and adapt, you're on your way.

KEY FACTORS IN CHANGING TECHNIQUES

Throughout this book we will be trying to separate discovery techniques into usable categories. We may call something an individual technique, however, which *you* can adapt to a class-wide technique or vice-versa. We may give you an idea in language arts which you see as something you can use in social studies. That's fine with us. The whole idea is to pick and choose, adapt and change, and explore and invent the best combinations for *your* class. This will allow your personalized discovery techniques to become smooth, practical, interchangeable tools working for *you*. .

You may, for example, decide to use certain techniques to integrate into your classroom those special events which occur during the school year. Things like national or local elections and community activities may not occur at the same time every year, and you may not wish the opportunity to go by. Saving some techniques just for these special occasions may prove of immense value to you.

Perhaps a true incident can show you the cohesiveness to which we have been referring. Let's look at what one classroom teacher did to heighten her class's discovery potential.

"E PLURIBUS UNUM"

When Gale Kelly got her first assignment as a fourth grade teacher, she was naturally delighted, and a little apprehensive. Her only previous experience had been in a departmentalized system, and she was now faced with the situation of a self-contained classroom.

When Gale entered her new room she was pleased to notice that there were several bookcases and a work table at the back of the room. Mentally, she selected *that* as the place for individualized work. She was familiar with both the Discovery Potential Guide and the Personal Preference Chart, and she used them to plan the physical layout of her room.

One of the first things she noticed was that the previous teacher had left a bird feeder outside the window. Assessing that it might be a distraction, but also believing that it had great potential as a learning device, Gale added "keeping the bird feeder" to the classroom list of tasks. She also decided that sometime during the school year she would add something to the curriculum about ornithology.

She had familiarized herself with the curriculum requirements and found she had great leeway in the planning of daily subject matter. Again relying on the Discovery Potential Guide, she found several places for the logical co-ordination of available materials and necessary activities.

In short, even though Gale was entering a teaching situation that was new for her, she had many guideposts on which she could rely to enable herself and her students to have a successful, educationally rewarding, and discovery-filled year.

Chapter 4

Using the Classroom
as a Resource
for the Discovering Child

One of the very fascinating statistics involved in education is the length of time a child spends in a classroom during his school career. The average child spends 14,040 hours in a classroom from first grade through the senior year of high school, and longer than that if he goes to kindergarten or takes extra courses. The resultant challenge to us, as educators, to make this time as interesting, productive and rewarding as possible is indeed awesome.

YOUR CLASS, YOUR ROOM,
THEIR DISCOVERY

Whenever books are written about the classroom or teaching techniques, the emphasis is always on the child. Perhaps this is as it should be, for if our main concern as teachers is not the benefit, growth and development of the child, then what is the purpose of education? However, we feel that something must be said about the teacher as well. The assumption that a teacher has nothing to do but guide Johnny and Mary and Billy to new exciting heights of learning can only be made by someone who has never been in a classroom. For every beautiful, delicate moment involving an awakening mind there are 50 moments devoted to locker keys, milk money, transportation cards, PA announcements and requests to go to the lavatory. There are times when the teacher is file clerk, supply sergeant, purchasing agent, tour guide, and a few hundred other job descriptions never included in the course on "Principles and Practices of Elementary Education."

Perhaps because our responsibilities are so broad, it has always been assumed that we must carry these burdens alone. Furthermore, there seem to be two opinions about the role of our classes as these "outside" tasks mount. The first is that children could not possibly understand what is going on, and the second is that the students should be occupied in some quiet, educational work should the teacher be unavoidably distracted from her role as their personal guide.

To both these positions we politely say, "Phooey!" As the cry today is for reality in curriculum, shouldn't we say something about the reality of a classroom? True, those tasks are your responsibility, but if you keep them to yourself are you not encouraging the falacious belief that all the child is responsible for is the filling of his mind with facts, data, and new skills within the framework of the expanded three R's? That's nonsense. A smooth-running classroom demands that everybody does his part. Unless children discover their part in shared responsibility, they have gained nothing. It is amazing how much even a first grader can understand about his role as part of a class if he is given structured responsiblity. Yet we continue to give paper routes to nine-year-olds while schools require that middle grade *teachers* fill out attendance cards. This is just a further example of a dichotomy between outside-of-school responsibilities and in-school duties which would be laughable were it not so tragic.

We are expected to save desks, blackboards, text books, windows, etc. from destruction while running model classrooms. Fine, but what about the kids? What do they get from that? If we are keeping our eye on the textbooks, why should they? Isn't rising vandalism merely a sign of lack of learned responsibility?

Let's see how we can integrate relevance, responsibility, and discovery into a real, working classroom. With careful planning we *can* instill in our students a real sense of their role in the scheme of things.

A BRIEF WORD ON DISCIPLINE–
DISCOVERY THROUGH BEHAVIOR

We are certain you have heard someone say, "She's a great disciplinarian," or, "He has great discipline—he tells his class to jump, and they ask how high!" Well, that's not what we mean when we talk about discipline. All those two statements show is that the teachers mentioned have exerted their power and authority over their students. Discipline, on the other hand, means that the child has internalized certain modes of behavior and adapted them to conform to the socially acceptable norms which the teacher desires within a classroom. In the first case, the students have gained nothing they can carry with them while in the second, they are discovering that they are responsible for their own actions and the consequences thereof.

Please understand that we must have rules in our classroom or there will be chaos. The trick lies in the kind of rules we set. Our first step in setting rules is to determine what our school policy is as defined in either student handbooks or administrative bulletins. For example, is gum chewing allowed or is it banned? Are children to line up or do they come into the class as they arrive at school? We now have the skeleton of our rules. The muscles and sinews can be found within the Personal Preference Chart (Chapter 3). From viewing that you might ascertain that you prefer a quiet, tightly structured classroom (which requires a particular set of rules) or it might become apparent that you prefer a free, mobile type of classroom (which calls for an entirely different set). Finally, the flesh and blood are added when the students who form your class arrive for school.

It is at this point that you will find the Discovery Potential Guide an essential tool. For example, questions 1, 2, 5, 6, 7 under General, 5 and 6 under Environmental, 7 and 8 under Materials, and 4, 5, 6, 7 under Developmental will show you the direction your class rules should take in order for your class to best "discover" self-discipline.

There are three main factors we must keep in mind in structuring our rules. First, we must understand what we are asking for when we set the rules of our room. The student must gain a real sense of responsibility by conforming to them. If he cannot, we have fostered frustration, anger, and lowered self-confidence. Second, if we want them to discover discipline, there must be realistic options. Failure to conform to what is expected must be met with logical, relevant consequences, not empty threats or out-of-proportion punishments. There must be a real reason for the option other than to display the teacher's control. Third, determine who will benefit from the rules. If we are the only ones (either through having supreme control or because we gain some kind of status by having the kind of classroom one can always enter and find quiet) then perhaps we should look at our motives. Classroom rules are there as a framework within which *all* members must function. Determine if the class will benefit by gaining a new discovery of responsible self-discipline.

CHECKLIST OF PITFALLS AND HOW TO AVOID THEM

We'd like to take some time and deal with five major pitfalls encountered in the classroom and how not only to avoid them but to get the most discovery potential out of them. First, the pitfalls themselves:

1. Office requirements vs. class time
2. Planned lessons vs. unusual class or outside activity
3. Scheduled activities vs. absenteeism and illness
4. A unit, for any reason, just does not work
5. The unexpected and the bizarre

Let's take them in order. The first pitfall is very common. There are times when a teacher's desk seems filled with forms and requirements from department heads, supervisors, guidance, and administration, that must be done immediately. As one teacher put it:

> I remember one day when I found myself with a request for any changes of address needed for a transportation

review, forms to be filled out for the American Red Cross Annual Fund Raising Drive, invitations to be given out for the next PTA meeting, a request for orders from TAB Books, and a requisition form for the next two months supplies! At the bottom of each set of papers was the request, "Please complete immediately and return to me." Complete immediately!!! Never mind about the 35 kids I had in front of me who were ready to start work, after, of course, they told me everything they did over the weekend!

This is a perfect example of the type of situation which can be "saved" merely by making students aware that such things really do happen. Make them a part of the tasks to be accomplished. Then, when a situation such as the one described does occur, the class can be made to feel important as *you and they* cooperate to get the work done so the lesson can eventually begin.

As far as the second pitfall is concerned, we all know that every once in a while something will happen, and that beautiful lesson plan will fly right out the window. Last year a teacher recounted this story to us:

> We had just begun a whole unit of math review preparatory to switching to a new math book. When they left school on Friday afternoon, they were working beautifully. When they returned Monday morning, however, they were like a colony of very active ants. Nothing would settle them down. The cause? The local Little League team (and most of my kids were either part of it or knew someone who was), was going to the National Championships in Williamsport. Knowing that the excitement would mount almost continually for the next six weeks (after all, how often do you have potential national champions in your room?), I was faced with the problem of keeping my lesson plans and my sanity intact. I found that merely by changing apples and oranges to hits and runs and the usual math problems to ones involving the distances between our town and Pennsylvania, the kids got their math and we were all happy.

Even if your case is not as dramatic as this, make every effort to *use* the unusual and make it a part of your teaching; make it an aid rather than a detriment.

Elementary school seems to be the incubator for every childhood epidemic from measels to the flu. If you have the slightest doubt of the disruptive force a circulating case of chicken pox can be, try planning your lessons around one. One teacher gave us a suggestion which she had found very successful. If an outbreak of something contagious occurs, she switches as much of her classwork to individualized testing and reviewing as she can. If new material must be introduced, it is done through mimeographed notes and ditto sheets. Anything that allows your students to get back in stride quickly saves you work and them the frustration of being behind.

This next pitfall is one that seems particularly touchy. Sometimes a unit just doesn't seem to jell. It is well thought out, carefully planned, has all the materials for motivation, but for one reason or another, the spark that ignites it is not there. This leads to two depressing alternatives: either the teacher gets angry at the class because they won't cooperate, or the class turns off because of the lack of enthusiasm. The answer may sound simplistic, but where does it say that once we start something we have to stick with it to the bitter end? We are not talking here of "necessary tediums" like memorizing spelling words or parts of speech, but if that great idea we had about teaching the way the pioneers cooked goes up in smoke (literally or figuratively), then either switch to an alternative method or wind it up and go on to something more enjoyable both for us and our students.

Finally, how do we deal with the unexpected, the bizarre? We'll spend some time later on talking about the myriad things that may unexpectedly happen in our class, but let's say a word here about some things to keep in mind. Many things are disruptive—fire drills, first snowfalls, sudden claps of thunder, wasps, and dogs. Remember that teacher reaction to the bizarre will be reflected in the student reaction. If something silly happens—laugh. This clears the air, makes a common bond, and as you gain control of yourself, so will your students. You may even find the shared experience a benefit later on. Anything that strengthens the bond between the teacher and the class is important. Make your pitfalls work *for* you.

BLUEPRINT FOR SEATING AND
ROOM ARRANGEMENT

Let's look at four major types of room arrangements:
1. Traditional (Figure 4-1)
2. Modular (Figure 4-2)
3. Arc (Figure 4-3)
4. Open Classroom (Figure 4-4)

In the traditional, or 5 x 5, classroom children sit in rows and work individually with the class working as a unit. Its advantages are that it is easily cared for, quiet, allows easy teacher access to students, and has clear sight lines. Its main disadvantage is its static nature. For group work seats must be "changed" and later returned to their proper positions. This may give the impression that group work is extraneous to "real" work which is done by the individual. It is commonly used in early primary and in individual skill work subjects such as math and spelling on all levels of academic achievement.

FIGURE 4-1

Traditional

In the modular arrangement, several seats are faced against each other with the work area shared by the students in it. Its advantages are the easy access to shared learning, the "helping" nature of the group, and increased work space. Its disadvantages are noise, poor teacher sight lines, difficulty in teacher and student mobility, and difficulty in working with the class as a whole. It has been well used in such investigative subjects as science and social studies and in middle grade classes within the middle achievement ranges.

FIGURE 4-2

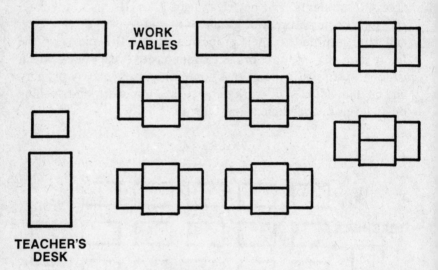

Modular

The arc is an arrangement where chairs are placed on sides of the room facing an inward area which is either open or contains the teacher's desk. The arc combines the advantages of the traditional and modular arrangements. It has good teacher sight lines, is quieter than the modular and easier to control, while each child is connected to others in his immediate circle and these overlap to connect individuals to more than one group.

Under disadvantages are the difficulty of teacher access to students, and the fact that it is a poor arrangement for testing. The arc works well in demonstration subjects such as art, music, science, drama, etc., and in late middle and upper grade classrooms, particularly for students in the high achievement range.

FIGURE 4-3

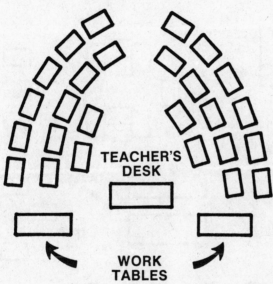

TEACHER'S DESK

WORK TABLES

Finally, there is the open classroom which has been described as organized chaos. The room is divided into areas, each having its own seating arrangement, some traditional, some modular, some arc-like, and work tables and areas. This can be done in a single classroom, but it is more conducive to an oversized or double room. Its advantages are that it allows for great flexibility of both teacher and student, and allows students to work at their own pace and explore on their own. The main disadvantages are that the moments of peace and quiet are rare if not non-existent, planning is done by subject matter and the class is never thought of as a whole, and it demands that the personality of the teacher and the maturity of the students balance correctly for best results. This setup works well in tract/level grouping, contract work and team teaching. It is probably most effective in the middle grades.

FIGURE 4-4

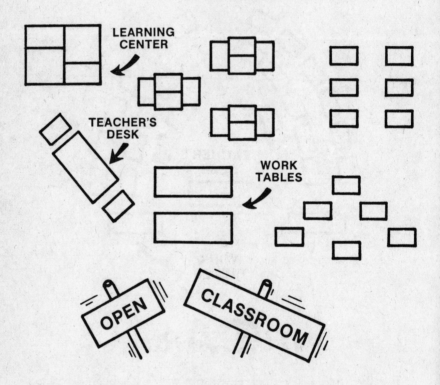

Now that we have described these four types of arrangements, go back and look at your Discovery Potential Guide and your Personal Preference Chart. Through the use of these forms, you have discovered what *you* wish to accomplish in your class. In choosing the type of seating arrangement for your room, make certain you select that arrangement which most closely parallels your goals and offers you the best chance for success. Create a millieu in which *you* can best work, and your class will begin to discover success.

Aside from seating arrangements, there are two other resources for aiding the developing child—the bulletin board and the class library.

HOW TO UTILIZE THE BULLETIN BOARD AS A DISCOVERY TECHNIQUE

Most every classroom has an area designated as the bulletin board. Whether it be cork, pressed board, or an empty piece of wall space, it is there. What are you going to do with it?

Well, what do *you* want *it* to do? Before you start working with it, decide what function you want this area to perform. We offer the following checklist of your options:

1. DISPLAY AREA—Teachers may use the bulletin board to display the student's work—compositions, reports, drawings, etc. Be careful not to hamper student growth by falling into common traps such as:
   a. Only perfect papers are put up. This discourages students from trying. Better to set a criteria of neatness, originality, etc.
   b. Student's work kept up too long. If you are using the display as an incentive, change it often.
   c. Displaying without reason. If you have a particular reason for putting a student's paper up there, make certain the student understands it.

In short, if you use the bulletin board as a display area, make sure that what you are displaying is the growth and success of your entire class.

2. PROPAGANDA BILLBOARD—Some teachers have found great success using the bulletin board to reinforce positive social values and spur their students to learn and grow. This may be done through sayings, slogans, inspirational pictures or cartoons. Keep these three guidelines in mind:
   a. At whom are they aimed? They shouldn't be for a few selected students, but something with which all your students can identify.
   b. Will your class understand? No matter how clever a cartoon may be, it is worthless if the students cannot understand its message.

c. What do you expect to be gained? Whatever the desired outcome, be sure it reinforces what you want it to. Check often to see if students are receiving the message being sent.

3. INFORMATION CENTER—When the bulletin board is used in this manner, announcements, charts, schedules, etc., are placed there. Even some advertisements and posters are seen. Be sure:
   a. They are relevant to your class.
   b. They are kept current by removing things that are past.
   c. The students *use* the board for their day to day needs. If, for example, the cafeteria's daily menu is posted, no student should have to ask you what is for lunch.

4. THE WORKING BOARD—This dynamic tool can be a great help as a discovery technique. It can be co-ordinated with a class project, used to show a student's progress toward a particular goal, or may be in and of itself a student responsibility. Some of the things you can do with this type of board are:
   a. Show the research done on the flags, outfits and weapons of the Revolutionary Army.
   b. A group of students may use the bulletin board to campaign for Mr. Lincoln vs. Mr. Douglas.
   c. A chart may be used to reinforce social development. For example, every time a child does something which shows good citizenship or responsibility, a star is placed next to his name. When the child has received ten stars, he is made office runner (or some other desired position) for a week.

Whatever the way in which we intend to utilize the bulletin board, let us realize the advantages inherent in this otherwise empty space. Let our students get the most out of it.

THE CLASS LIBRARY—
A DYNAMIC TOOL

It is difficult not to overemphasize the importance of a class library. A class library is simply that, a library for use by our class in the classroom and their homes. This dynamic tool has so many uses that to teach without one would seem like teaching without a blackboard or textbooks. There is not a classroom anywhere that should be deprived of this learning device.

If your school is affluent enough, you can equip your library with three sections:

    A. A resource section with a set of encyclopedias, several dictionaries, almanacs, atlases, etc.

    B. A reading section made up of books either bought or donated dealing with the myriad things found in your class's curriculum.

    C. An easy come, easy go section that contains magazines, books, comics, etc., that children can bring in, exchange, keep, etc., and are just for fun.

Even in our most economically depressed areas there are resources open to teachers through book clubs, publishing companies, charities, and federal programs for the gathering of reading materials for use in the classroom.

A class library can be set up anywhere. The place most often chosen is a bookcase in the back of the room, but we have seen cinder block and plank bookshelves along walls, brick bookend window-sill shelves, and even a brightly painted upended orange crate. As long as it is bright, enticing, and attractive, it can be any place where the students can have access to it.

Teachers find two basic uses for a class library: it is either an information center where students can learn on their own, and/or it is a recreational area where students develop reading skills, love of reading, and self-discipline concerning the use of time. Both of these are valid and may be used interchangably. Since part of our definition of discovery is the constant quest to learn more, we have found the class library a very rewarding and ongoing asset.

The hardest thing in setting up a class library is selecting reading material and making sure that the students get the most out of it. This difficulty can be overcome by determining the reading levels of your class (you found that out in the Discovery Potential Guide.), the interests of various members of your class, and how *you* feel about class and student responsibility (see your Personal Preference Chart). Remember, the more often you interweave the class library into your lesson plans and class activities, the more interest the students will take in it and the more integral a part of their classroom environment it will become.

The class library in the elementary school classroom must rank at the top of the requirements for making your classroom the primary resource for the developing child.

"THE MOVING DESK"

"Well," said Mr. Harvey, an eighth grade teacher, "it's time to go move my desk again. See you later."

When he had left the teacher's room we asked what he had meant.

"Our school year is divided into four marking periods," another teacher explained, "and at the start of each marking period Mr. Harvey moves his desk so it's against a different wall of his classroom, and the kids turn their desks to face him. He's done it for as long as I've known him."

Curious, we sought out Mr. Harvey later in the day and asked him if he had any specific reasons for his moving desk.

"I certainly do," he answered. "For one thing, I make sure that every spring the students have their backs facing the windows, and that cuts down on daydreaming. Also the change in seating is a very real thing, and coming when it does, it has the effect of saying, 'O.K., one phase of your eighth grade life has finished and another is beginning.' My kids know that if they've done poorly during the past marking period, that's over, and they can start new and fresh, putting the past behind them and working toward the future. It also serves warning that if a student has been doing well, he can't let up or coast, because we're starting fresh.

"Also, I can have the class face that part of the room I'll be using most during that marking period. For instance, they're facing the bulletin board when I'm doing my propaganda unit, and in June, when I show a lot of films, they're facing the wall screen. Oh, and there's one other reason."

"What's that?" we asked.

"The kids like it."

As long as there are teachers who think and plan keeping in mind what is best for their class's growth, there will be real education taking place in America's classrooms. Use what you have learned about your class and yourself to build and to turn your classroom into a resource for the child and you will have done your students a service that will be of benefit to them throughout their lives.

Chapter 5

Discovery Techniques and Activities That Unlock Behavioral Hang-ups

---

Nothing impedes the progress of education like a behavioral problem. The student who acts up or otherwise presents behavioral difficulties is a real and present danger, for his actions halt the education not only of himself, but of others as well. In our book *Personalized Behavioral Modification: Practical Techniques for Elementary Educators*[1], we outlined a school-wide plan for dealing with behavioral problems as they really exist in schools throughout the nation. Let's see how we may apply these principles in discovery techniques that deal effectively with the classroom behavioral problem.

UNDERSTANDING BEHAVIORAL PATTERNS

All behavior is caused. You won't find many people who will disagree with that statement. If, as teachers, we can discover the causes for most negative behavior, perhaps we can begin to channel our discovery techniques toward solutions rather than merely punishments which have a tendency to treat the symptom rather than the disease.

We have found that there are eight major types of misconduct prevalent in a classroom. They are:

    1. CLASSROOM DISTRACTIONS—talking, excessive movement, interruptions, etc.

---

[1]P. Susan Mamchak with Steven R. Mamchak, *Personalized Behavioral Modification: Practical Techniques for Elementary Educators,* Parker Publishing Co., West Nyack, N. Y., 1976.

2. ASSAULT ON PERSONS—minor skirmishes to major brawls.

3. ASSAULT ON PROPERTY—from writing in a book to major vandalism.

4. CHARACTER VIOLATIONS—cheating, lying, tattling, etc.

5. REBELLION—from refusal to do the assigned task to talking back to the teacher.

6. SEASONAL/REGIONAL—seasonal changes and the location of your school may bring their own inherent problems—snowball fights or the opening of hunting season for example.

7. SMOKING—just because it's an elementary school doesn't mean that this can't be a problem.

8. COMMUNITY RELATED—those problems which break community as well as school rules—false fire alarms and drug possession, for example.

We have further discovered that there are five major reasons for misconduct. They are:

1. ATTENTION GETTING—of teacher, peers, or parents.

2. REVENGE—to get back at someone for a real or imagined wrong.

3. PEER ACCEPTANCE—if he does "it," he'll be accepted.

4. IMPROVING SELF-IMAGE—he does something to see if he is brave or clever enough to get away with it.

5. HIDDEN CAUSES—there is no *apparent* reason why he does it.

The type of misconduct is obvious as soon as you observe it, but how do you discover the reasons a child acts as he does? The obvious answer might be to ask him. Go right ahead, if you want to find out how fertile an imagination can be, but don't rely on the answers as the final word. It would be better to have something a bit more objective.

Let's assume you are sitting at your desk when a fight begins in your classroom. O.K., you're now faced with number 2 on the list of types, ASSAULT ON PERSONS. You break up the fight, and are now faced with determining the reason for it. The two combatants are still making nasty noises at each other, but there has been no major damage. O.K., what do you do, King Solomon?

We have found that any one of the three following techniques will bring about the double result of discovering the cause and getting the class back in order:

GO TO YOUR RESPECTIVE CORNERS—Each combatant is given a piece of paper, sent to the opposite side of the classroom, and given a three minute time limit in which to write down why *the other guy* should get in trouble. At the end of the time, the papers are exchanged and the combatants given three more minutes to defend themselves against the charges. By the end of the six minutes the kids are usually calmed down, and the teacher has had time to get the class back in order. She takes the papers and the kids outside, reads them, asks clarifying questions if needed, and can usually determine the causes. REMEMBER, this is not a solution, it merely ascertains causes and calms everyone down.

EQUAL TIME—This technique works for younger children. Send them to opposite sides of the room as before, but this time with crayons, paper, and instructions to draw a picture of themselves and the way they feel *right now.* While this is being done you can calm down the class. Now take each child outside *separately,* look at the drawing (which invariable depicts sadness or hostility), and comment along the lines of, "This person looks sad/angry. Why is he?" Don't refer to the fight. Eventually, causes and motives will become known.

THE BRIEF—Proceed as in the first technique, except that they don't exchange papers, and they are only to write their views of their guilt or innocence in terms of the situation. This is not a separate technique, although it does allow you to calm down the class and determine causes, but should be used in conjunction with THE STUDENT COURT which will be described later in this chapter.

Any technique which will determine causes is a valid one. You may use the above techniques with many other types of misbehavior as well.

If, along with seeking after causes, we keep a record of infractions, when they occur, on what days, during what subjects, involving whom, etc. (see Figure 5-1 for a sample page from a teacher's notebook), we may see a pattern of misbehavior forming. From Figure 5-1 can you determine any patterns? Does it become apparent that most fights involve Billy R. and occur on Monday mornings after Billy has been at home all weekend? Might this suggest a possible way of helping Billy?

Determining patterns and causes is our first step, but now we must work toward their solution. Here, you will find that a very useful tool is empathy.

HOW TO UTILIZE EMPATHY
IN DISCOVERY TECHNIQUES

You are traveling backward now, back to the days when you were a child. You're in school, and everything is big and you are small. Think for a moment; make an effort to remember what it was like. Everyone has a say about you, except you. And now you have done something wrong. The teacher is calling you up to the front of the room. She is at least 100 feet taller than you are, and when she looks down, you feel like that fly you saw get stuck on the fly paper.

Now come back to being a teacher. How do you feel about that "you" as a child? That is the way you should feel when dealing with all your behavioral problems. The child "you" doesn't want or need to be badgered, scared, belittled, or threatened with unnamed terrors; the teacher "you" must be careful to do none of these.

When using any of the discovery techniques in this book, whether on behavior or any other aspect of school life, keep in mind the child's point of view. Be aware of what you are asking in relationship to what the child can do. Through the Discovery Potential Guide you have already determined age, maturity, and aptitude levels. Don't expect a first grader to act like a third

FIGURE 5-1

TIME OF DAY	DAY OF THE WEEK	SUBJECT BEING TAUGHT AT THE TIME	STUDENTS INVOLVED	TYPE OF MIS-CONDUCT	CAUSE	NOTES
10:15	MON.	READING	BILLY R. TOM W.	FIGHT	REVENGE?	3RD FIGHT FOR B.R.
11:27	MON.	RECESS	BILLY R. JIM M.	FIGHT	REVENGE - PEER ACCEPT.	
1:15	TUES.	MATH	KATHY H.	PAPER AIRPLANE	ATTENTION GETTING	
2:05	THURS.	MATH	DANIEL S. JUDY K.	CONSTANT TALKING	"	
10:53	FRI.	SCIENCE	DON P.	CHEATING ON TEST	SELF-IMAGE	
9:22	MON.	ENGLISH	KEN B. BILLY R.	FIGHT	HIDDEN?	WOULDN'T TALK ABOUT IT
10:41	MON.	SOC. STUD.	BILLY R.	THROWING ERASERS	ATTENTION GETTING	
2:46	MON.	ART	GEORGIA D.	THREW PAINT	REVENGE	STUPID REACTION TO INSULT
12:54	WED.	LUNCH	DOUG H.	SMOKING	PEER ACCEPTANCE	
1:17	FRI.	RECESS	BILLY R.	PUSHED MARY SHE FELL	HIDDEN	DISPROPORTIONATE OVER-REACTION
11:05	MON.	RECESS	BILLY R. JOE C.	FIGHT	REVENGE	VERY VIOLENT!
1:21	TUES.	MATH	DANIEL S.	PUT TACK ON CHAIR	ATTENTION - PEER ACCEPT.	
2:13	THURS.	MUSIC	MARY LOU P.	OBSCENITY	REVENGE	1ST INCIDENT - LOST TEMPER
9:57	MON.	READING	BILLY R. TOM W.	FIGHT	HIDDEN	NO APPARENT CAUSE???
10:18	MON.	SOC. STUD.	BILLY R.	THREW BOOK OUT WINDOW	REVENGE?	GETTING BACK AT ME?
1:33	WED.	RECESS	DON P.	SMOKING	PEER ACCEPT.	
1:54	WED.	RECESS	DANIEL S. SUE P.	LET AIR OUT OF VOLLYBALL	"	TOOK A DARE - CLASS CLOWN?
12:01	THURS.	LUNCH	KEN B. DOUG H.	FIGHT	REVENGE	SILLY ARGUMENT BETWEEN FRIENDS
3:04	FRI.	GYM	BILLY R.	REFUSED TO PLAY	ATTENTION?	
10:01	MON.	READING	BILLY R. JIM M.	FIGHT	REVENGE	WHY ALWAYS ON MONDAY???
11:12	TUES.	SOC. STUD.	JOE C.	RIPPED TEXTBOOK	ATTENTION GETTING	
1:58	WED.	RECESS	DON P.	SMOKING	PEER ACCEPT.	

grader, and conversely, don't treat a seventh grader like a fourth grade student.

If we maintain a high level of empathy in dealing with our children, we will find that they will respond, and we will have accomplished more toward their growth and development than any number of detentions, compositions, or stern talks could ever hope to do. We will be well on our way if we maintain empathy and at the same time remain firm, fair, and, above all, fast.

IMMEDIACY— A TEACHER'S BEST FRIEND

Whenever a problem occurs it is best to have a plan of action that can be implemented *immediately*. The philosophy of "Wait till your father gets home!" transplanted to the classroom has the negative effect of separating cause and effect. Punishment should not be a threat. It should, if it is to be effective, be the natural outgrowth of the misconduct. If you do A, then B will follow. Not just if the the teacher is in a bad mood, but *always*.

If your rules have been carefully thought out to coincide with socially acceptable norms and not merely personal whims, then you have also determined what you think the result of the abrogation of those rules should be. If these are explained to the students along with the rules, and if you are consistent, then you have built in immediacy of action. For example, Mary writes in a textbook. You have stated that anyone who disfigures property shall be responsible for cleaning all the desks in the room. Consequently, Mary cleans the desks! Even if she won't be doing the task until after school, she and the rest of the class still understand that the behavior has brought about the punitive action. Also, it doesn't matter if Mary is the best-loved or worst-liked student in the class, for under such a system it is impossible for the teacher to play favorites, either positively or negatively.

While it is impossible that all actions be carried out at once, during class time, the teacher should have a few options open for handling things *right now*. These, too, should be clearly described and defined to your class. Of course, there can be some specials up your sleeve that will serve in very special cases.

Let's look at some ways in which teachers have filled the need for immediacy of action:

1. A child cannot work in a group—He is permitted to use the resources of the class library to work independently on the same material.
2. A child refuses to allow the class to continue with a lesson—He is removed from the group, but not the classroom, for a certain amount of time to work in the individual work area.
3. A child repeatedly distracts those around him—He has his seat changed for a specified length of time.

In some cases, the simple converse of a rule may prove the most valuable remedy. For instance, if you have stated that they may get up and sharpen pencils whenever they like, and Sandy has sharpened her pencil 15 times in the last 5 minutes while the class is trying to study, you might say, "Sandy, you are not handling your responsibility for using the pencil sharpener very well, so for the next hour you may not sharpen your pencil unless you ask me first. After that you'll be on your own again." This loss of freedom of action is directly related to the offense and beneficial to Sandy's development.

HOW TO SCRATCH "THE ITCH"

The scene of the leather-jacketed student wielding a switchblade knife and backing a teacher into a corner may pack 'em in at the local movie house, but how often have *you* seen it happen? More often, teachers are faced with things like the constant talker, the spitball thrower, the paper airplane manufacturer, the knuckle cracker, and other "itches." We know who they are—we need no further description. What we need is a plan for dealing with them.

We offer for your consideration a unique plan, beautifully conceived, ultimately practical, and an invaluable tool for allowing the teacher to help students discover the value of social responsibility. It is the brainchild of Carlether P. Roy who uses it with her classes. We'll let her describe it to you. We've called it:

THE STUDENT COURT—"Within the first week of school, criteria of conduct and the compensation for infractions are decided upon by the entire class and the teacher—that is, how the students should comport themselves in the lunchroom, playground, halls, library, classrooms, etc.—in short, any social situation. The teacher *and* the students then select a team to review any infractions. The team and the teacher meet and discuss the importance of setting up the 'declaration system.' A student who commits an infraction must meet with the team for a review of his/her involvement. It is then incumbent upon the team to determine whether the student's involvement is serious enough to require a 'declaration' and the consequences.

"Directly facing the pressure of peers as well as the right to express his or her misuse of time, energy, good judgement, and consideration for others leads to more thoughtful action in future situations. Also, the confrontation by peers who disapprove or question various forms of behavior makes the learning process all the more real.

"The process is as follows: After the child has stated his case, the team decides what shall be done. If they judge it serious enough, it may require a 'declaration' (see Figure 5-2). They will also decide a compensation for the violation. The student must agree to the declaration and sign it. After a designated time, the team reviews the case, decides whether or not the student has fulfilled the requirement, and, if so, issue a Follow Up Report (see Figure 5-3) showing their approval of his 'rehabilitation.'

"This technique can be effective providing the teacher *really* includes the committee of students. It should begin within the first month of school. The process can be effective *only* when all concerned follow up properly. The use of the technique proved effective in four out of five cases of students who were disciplined by its use. Ineffectiveness as a result of using the technique was encountered only in the following circumstances: The teacher became too busy to follow through, and student's individual problems were too intense for handling in the classroom."

FIGURE 5-2

DECLARATION OF VIOLATION

Student_____ Age_____

Date_____ Grade_____

INFRACTION:_____

_____

EXPLANATION OF INCIDENT:_____

_____

_____

CHOICE OF COMPENSATION FOR VIOLATION:

_____Remain after school 1 day _____2 days _____

_____Write a note of apology

_____Offer an oral apology

_____Accept responsibility for helping to improve behavior in the area of violation

_____Write a story about myself. Tell why I acted this way.

_____   _____
        Student   Teacher

_____

_____
                    Investigating Team

FIGURE 5-3

FOLLOW UP REPORT

_____has fulfilled the requirement as indicated on the Declaration of Violation form.

    The undersigned accept his ____her ____effort to improve his ____her ____behavior.

    We further recommend that _____
should exercise better self-control and avoid appearing before this committee for at least three months.

                               _____

                               _____

                               _____

                               _____

                               _____

                               Teacher

Whether you decide to use this technique or one of your own which you have found to be effective, be certain to keep it fair, consistent, and graded—that is, simple consequences for simple violations to more complex punitive actions for repeated or more involved infractions. Also, as in Carlether P. Roy's technique, the time limits should be realistic. A September offender cannot be expected to be good until June. If he can behave until "next week," he will have discovered success, and that may well trigger other successes.

We cannot leave this section without a word about a particularly "itchy" problem and a technique for handling it. The problem comes from the child who tattles, and the solution comes from Dr. Lonnie Carton of the professorial staff of Tufts University and broadcast journalist for the CBS network.

When a child comes up to you and begins tattling, repeat exactly what is said without any inflection on your part. For example, Janie comes running up saying, "Peter stole Bobby's pencil!" You repeat flatly, "Peter stole Bobby's pencil ... " "Yeah," she continues, " and then he broke it!" "And then he broke it," you state. You ask no questions, you show no disapproval or approval. Tattling is mainly an attention getter, and by talking with the child you have given the attention, but it is a boring exchange, and one not likely to be repeated. We've tried it, and it works!

Although most of the teacher's time is spent with this type of problem, there may be some incidents which are so out of the ordinary that they will require special handling.

BLUEPRINT FOR HANDLING
THE BIZARRE

The bizarre, as we define it, falls into three categories:
1. EMOTIONAL OUTBURST—crying, shouting obscenities, holding his breath, etc. The child has lost control, but is not so far gone as to warrant removal.
2. PHYSICAL—Anything that physically happens to one child and affects the class: vomiting, epileptic seizure, major accident, etc.
3. COMPLETE IRRATIONALITY—The child is a danger to himself and others. He must be removed for the good of the class.

To remove a child from class may solve *your* problem for the moment, it does nothing to solve *the child's* problem unless there is sufficient follow-up. Consequently, you should always remember that *removal from class is a last resort.* Now let's look at our categories and see how they may be handled.

When faced with an EMOTIONAL OUTBURST by a child, consider what you would do if the child were an adult. When an adult is upset, we try to calm him down and *then* get at the causes. It should be no different with a child. To make light of a child's tears or to demand silence from an angered child simply does no good. If a child has lost control, it is *essential* that we keep ours. *First,* calm him down—give him something to do or send him to the lavatory until he's regained control. Later, after you have calmed the rest of the class without any reference to the outburst, you can deal with the child individually, either at your desk or in the hallway, and seek for causes and possible remedies *then.* We have found that by handling the situation in this manner, the frequency of such outbursts decreases, and the other children learn by example how to handle emotional outbursts in others.

With PHYSICAL difficulties, it is a case of preventive medicine. Early in the year, when you are explaining the procedures for your class, you set up and explain procedures for handling physical problems. You might try this technique:

> DRILL—"If we should have an accident," the teacher said to the class, "or someone gets sick, everyone is to go to his desk and sit down. That makes it easy for us to help the person. Danny, don't wait for me to tell you, you go to the nurse and tell her to come here. Alice, if Danny isn't here, you go. Don't run, just walk fast. Bobby, Mark, Steve, and Joan (Here are chosen the children who would most benefit from having something to do in an emergency), you watch everything that happens so if anyone asks, you can tell. Grace, you listen to me, and if I need anything, you get it for me. Jeff, you're Grace's backup. Shall we try a practice drill?"

These procedures should be drilled at least once every month. Additional procedures can also be worked out for the playground, halls, gym, etc. When everyone has something specific to do, there is no panic, and the children learn responsibility.

When faced with COMPLETE IRRATIONALITY, and you have tried everything, the child may, indeed, need to be removed from class. What we must remember when we *remove* a child is that eventually, he will have to *return.* It must be fully understood by him and by the class that it was the *behavior* that caused the removal—not the child, not our whim, but the *action.* It must be made clear that what you will not tolerate is throwing a chair across the room, *not* Billy who threw the chair. Once you have decided, make the removal as quick as possible. Send him to the office *first*; write out the discipline form *later*. If, when you went over the rules with your class, you outlined precisely what were removable offences (and they should be very few), take the opportunity as soon as the child has left to go over these rules again. It would also be wise, later in the day, to see the child and explain this to him as well. Make it clear, both to the violator and the class, that *Billy* is welcome back, his *behavior* is not. The children have gained a sense of justice, and even Billy may begin to understand.

We believe that "once misbehaving students are shown *how* to change, given encouragement to *try* their new tools for change, and receive beneficial, *positive* reinforcement *while* they are changing, the goal of socially acceptable behavior is achieved."[2] Gear your discovery techniques to these principles, and you will find that the carry-over is tremendous.

"I LIKE YOU, BUT YOUR BEHAVIOR STINKS"

We devote this last section on behavior to a teacher who understood the difference between the student and the behavior through a technique she calls:

> THE ACTOR—"Sherri, you've told me that the class doesn't like you, and you know what, I believe you. I've watched; I can see it. I agree with you, something has to be done. Tell you what, let's do some detective work. Let's take just the kids around your seat. For two days, we're gonna leave 'em alone. Don't touch anything of theirs, don't look at their books, don't even talk to them unless they talk to you first. Oh, and when you do talk to them, make sure you say things like "Please," and "Thank you." Then, if anything happens with them and you, it's gonna have to be their fault. We'll compare notes on Friday.

---

[2]Ibid.

Remember, for this to work, you gotta really act like a straight kid, and you can't tell 'em anything about this conversation or they'll get wise."

For two days, Sherri was the model student. While the kids didn't fall in love with her, there were no incidents, and, thanks to some private work on the part of the teacher, there had been some minor positive responses. On Friday, the teacher met with Sherri again.

During the conversation, Sherri remarked, "Gee, I helped Mary Lou with her homework instead of tearing it up like I did before, and when I sat next to her at lunch, she didn't move away. You know, Bobby didn't call me 'icky' once in two whole days. Jimmy's still bein' a rat!" "O.K.," said the teacher "let's do a number on Jimmy. Keep up what you've been doing, it's great. Now what do you think we can do to bring Jimmy into line . . . "

In her attempt to modify the behavior of those around her by "acting" good, Sherri never realized that she was, indeed, modifying her own behavior. The successes were her own, and aided by the positive reinforcement of the teacher, Sherri was developing a new pattern of behavioral success. Later, when Sherri is secure in her new "character," she and the teacher will review the progress she has made, and the steps *Sherri* took to get there. This realization, combined with Sherri's tangible success, will be the foundation of her new, permanent growth in behavior.

Chapter 6

Teaching Basic Skills
With Discovery Techniques
in Your Classroom

The "Basic Skills" are the *sine qua non* of learning. Before we get into specific subject areas, therefore, we would like to spend some time pinpointing *your* class's needs. We will be using the references you have already placed in your notebook, and we'll be adding a few pages. If you're ready, let's begin.

UNDERSTANDING SKILLS, GRADES, INTERESTS, AND KIDS

When we have decided to introduce new material to our classes and are looking for the best discovery techniques to help them, where do you think we should start in order to determine our chances of success? How many of you said the Discovery Potential Guide? Well, you're absolutely right. Let's see how.

In filling out the Discovery Potential Guide, you filled out five very important statements concerning your class:

1. How it is grouped
2. Its grade level
3. Its achievement level (Apptitude/IQ)
4. Physical ability (motor co-ordination)
5. Reading ability (under/on/above grade level)

With these you have been able to generalize about your class.

91

Now we are going to give you two new factors which will help add specificity to your information. They are:

1. The Social Diagram (Figure 6-1) and its attendant chart (Figure 6-2)
2. The Skill Chart (Figure 6-3) and its attendant chart (Figure 6-4)

The Discovery Potential Guide and its companion piece, the Personal Preference Chart are of most value when completed within two weeks of the start of school. Once completed, they remain unchanged although they are referred to many times. The Social Diagram and the Skill Chart are also made out within the first month of school, but they continue to be revised approximately once every five weeks by the teacher, right on through to June. If we do this, we will find that student growth, direction, and the types of material we need to reach him will be so carefully pinpointed that we will find our teaching has gained in intensity and efficiency. Furthermore, as one teacher put it, "The shock of having physical, tangible evidence that something positive is really happening in the class is a real shot in the arm for my sometimes flagging enthusiasm."

Now let's take a look at each of these devices and see just how invaluable they can be in increasing your understanding of student needs and keeping your discovery techniques on target.

The Social Diagram. The purpose of this form is to determine the precise *social development* of each child in your class in each of sixteen major categories.

Look at Figure 6-1. Down the left-hand side of the paper are listed sixteen categories of social development. Across the top are listed (by you) the names of all the children in your class, one to a column. You now go down the list for each child and evaluate his development in each category. For our purposes we developed a number system, with each number indicating a stage of development:

1. Extremely well developed
2. Shows good progress toward developing
3. Average (sometimes yes, sometimes no)
4. Needs help developing
5. Definite problem area

FIGURE 6-1

THE SOCIAL DIAGRAM

CATEGORY	Tom W.	Joe E.	Alice H.	Rory A.	Bill W.	Bob P.	Jane R.	Patty H.	Sue P.	Steve M.	George P.	Mary B.	Cindy T.
Leadership	3	3	1	2	3	(5)	2	4	3	4	1	4	(5)
Dependability	3	(5)	1	1	2	4	3	(5)	3	3	1	4	(5)
Sense of Fairness	2	(5)	1	3	1	4	4	3	2	3	2	(5)	(5)
Ability to Share	3	4	3	2	1	3	(5)	3	1	4	2	4	4
Honesty	2	(5)	1	2	3	2	(5)	4	1	3	1	3	(5)
Ability to Work Alone	1	4	3	1	3	3	4	3	3	1	1	2	3
Ability to Work in Groups	2	(5)	1	4	3	3	2	3	1	3	1	3	4
Compassion	3	4	2	3	3	4	3	3	1	1	2	2	(5)
Sense of Proportion and Appropriateness	4	(5)	2	3	2	2	2	3	2	2	1	2	4
Courteousness	3	(5)	1	2	4	4	3	2	2	1	1	2	(5)
Respect for Adults/Authority	4	(5)	1	3	4	3	3	3	1	1	2	2	(5)
Awareness of World Around Him/Her	3	4	3	2	2	3	2	3	2	1	2	3	
Self Awareness and Role	4	4	1	2	3	2	2	3	1	2	1	2	4
Self-discipline	4	(5)	1	3	3	3	4	3	2	3	1	4	(5)
Understands/Respects Private Property	2	(5)	1	4	3	3	3	2	2	1	2	3	(5)
Responsibility	4	(5)	1	3	4	3	3	3	1	2	1	4	(5)

For example, let's take Leadership. Tom is always at the fore, and the other children look to him for direction—assign him a one in that category. Dick sometimes just goes along, but occasionally comes up with something that causes the class to follow him—possibly a three. Harry, on the other hand, seems a born follower and never volunteers for anything or suggests anything—most likely five.

If you are thinking that this is very subjective, you're right, it is. Consider, however, that you, as their teacher, spend a goodly part of your day with them, day in and day out, and are intimately involved with their development. Who better to make out the chart? Besides, this chart is to help you help your students and no one besides you will see it.

In any case, once you are finished your chart should look somewhat like the one in Figure 6-1. Go back over it now and circle each five you come to. Once you have completed this task you will be ready to go on to the next step.

Look at Figure 6-2. Again, list the categories down the left-hand margin. Now divide the space to the right of the categories with vertical lines, each line representative of a unit of five. (See Figure 6-2 for clarification.) Go back to your first form, and go across horizontally for each category, counting the number of students to whom you assigned a three, four or five. When you have determined this number, make an appropriate mark on the diagram chart and color in the space from zero to that number. When you have finished, yours should look like Figure 6-2, with, of course, the necessary differences for your class.

The immense value of both these forms should now become obvious. By studying the Social Diagram Chart you can tell what areas of social development need the most work in *your* particular class. You can also tell how to approach each area. If only three students need development in honesty, for example, it would best be handled on an individual basis; if the number is seven through ten, perhaps small group work would be best; if it's something like 20, however, better plan a classwide attack. Also, when you are doing individual work, a glance at the Social Diagram will tell you precisely those students who need the most help (you circled all the fives, remember?).

FIGURE 6-2

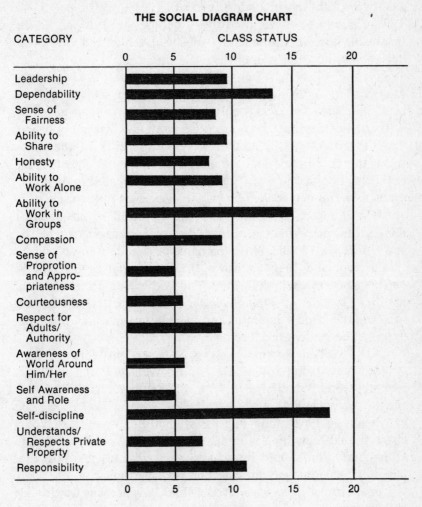

THE SOCIAL DIAGRAM CHART

If you fill out these charts every five weeks, as we indicated earlier, you will have the additional benefit of being able to tell progress both individually and on a classwide basis. In a second you can tell if Alice has become better or worse in any given category, if the class as a whole has improved in any given category, and what potential problems are beginning to develop for individual students and for the class. Armed with this knowledge, you can quite often get to a trouble spot *before* it becomes a problem and select the most effective methods for dealing with those which already exist.

Teachers who have used this method have found it an invaluable tool in the teaching of social values and the social development of their students.

The Skill Chart. The purpose of the Skill Chart is to ascertain each child's individual command of various skills, and to determine areas of *class* retentions and reinforcement needs as well as the thrust of new teaching methods. The pinpointing benefit is twofold: First, the two opposite ends of the spectrum, the gifted child and the underachiever, come into the full spotlight, and second, the type of activity indicated (individual, group, class) is determined by the precise needs of the class.

Look at Figure 6-3. There you will see listed various component skills under the general headings of Language Arts, Math, and Conceptual Skills. Write the name of a student in your class at the top, and then go down the list evaluating the child's performance in each skill area. You will evaluate them with a number (1, 2, 3, or 4) and a letter (A, B, or C). The numbers indicate the child's potential, and the letter indicates the type of work the student produces:

1.—Excellent Potential   A.—Excellent Work
2.—Very Good Potential   B.—Average Work
3.—Good Potential   C.—Below Average Work
4.—Average Potential

When you have done this for students in your class, your chart should look something like Figure 6-3. Now by studying your chart, you should be able to gain great insights into the individual students in your class and their particular needs.

For example, if we have rated a child 1-A, perhaps we should be looking into enrichment activities for him, as there is a good chance he may be a gifted child. If a child were rated 4-A, he is probably working at his optimum. A 4-B or 3-B is most likely normal for his stage of development but could probably be urged to do somewhat better. A 1-B or 2-B would be the most likely candidates for special skill work to spur their productivity, while a 1-C most definitely needs work immediately; possibly he is an underachiever.

FIGURE 6-3

THE SKILL CHART

	TOMMY J.	AMY K.	BILLY Y.	JACK R.	LYNN S.	GAIL M.
LANGUAGE ARTS						
Spelling	2-B	1-A	4-C	2-A	3-C	1-B
Punctuation	3-c	1-B	4-B	2-A	3-c	2-c
Capitalization	4-B	1-A	3-B	2-A	3-B	1-c
Phonics	2-c	1-A	4-c	1-A	3-B	1-B
Word Recognition	3-B	2-B	4-c	2-A	3-c	2-c
Vocabulary	3-B	1-B	4-c	1-A	3-B	2-c
Dictionary/Encyclopedia Use	3-c	1-A	3-B	2-A	2-B	1-B
Penmanship	4-c	2-B	2-A	2-B	3-c	1-c
Composition	4-c	1-A	4-c	2-A	3-c	2-B
Sentence Structure	3-c	1-A	3-c	2-A	3-c	2-B
MATH						
Addition	1-A	1-A	3-B	2-A	2-A	1-A
Subtraction	1-A	1-A	3-B	1-A	2-A	1-A
Division — One Digit	1-A	1-A	4-c	2-A	2-A	1-B
Division — Two Digit	2-B	1-A	4-c	2-B	2-B	1-c
Multiplication — One Digit	1-A	1-A	4-c	2-A	2-B	1-B
Multiplication — Two Digit	2-B	1-B	4-c	2-B	2-c	1-c
Word Problems	4-B	1-A	4-c	1-B	3-c	2-B
Percentage	3-B	1-B	4-c	2-B	2-c	2-c
Fractions	3-B	1-c	4-c	2-c	2-c	3-c
Currency	2-A	1-A	3-B	1-A	2-A	1-B
Decimals/Metric	4-c	1-B	3-B	2-B	2-B	2-B
Measurements/Time	1-A	1-A	3-B	1-A	2-A	1-c
Shapes/Dimensions	3-B	1-c	2-B	2-c	1-A	3-c
CONCEPTUAL SKILLS						
Inductive Reasoning	3-c	1-B	2-B	2-c	4-c	1-A
Deductive Reasoning	2-c	1-A	2-B	2-A	4-c	1-A
Can Follow A Series Of At Least Three Directions	1-A	1-A	1-B	1-A	3-c	1-A
Can Apply A Set of Facts To More Than One Situation	3-c	1-A	2-B	2-B	4-c	1-A

Areas of need become even more definable when we apply what we have learned to the diagram in Figure 6-4. As we did for social development, count the number of children who have been assigned a 3-C or 4-C on the Skill Chart and graph that number on the Skill Chart Diagram (Figure 6-4 shows what this would look like for a typical class). Now, if we look at any particular skill area, we will be able to tell what kind of techniques are best for helping children improve within it. If it is a problem for only one through four students, then individualized techniques would work best; if five through sixteen students share the problem, small group work would prove most effective; if, however, it is anywhere from 17-25, then it is a class problem and should be approached by classwide techniques.

FIGURE 6-4

THE SKILL CHART

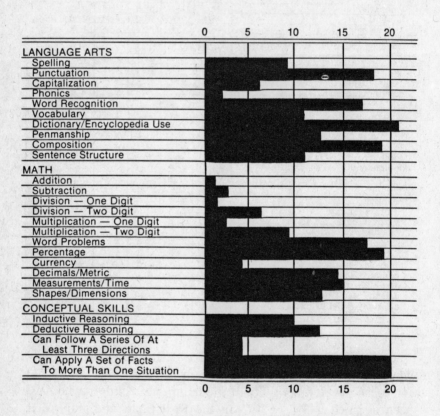

Of course, we are generalizing, for we have no way of knowing the particular set of circumstances attendant on *your* class. We, for example, have assumed an average size of 25 students, *you* may have more or less. Also, there may be other circumstances which affect your particular class that will have a bearing on what *you* do. *You know your class best.* With these charts and diagrams, however, you have an invaluable tool. Yes, they take some time to fill out, but it is time enormously well spent, for once done they will show you precise areas of need in particular detail both individually and class-wide, and they will suggest and help you determine the precise techniques which have the best chance of success. And *that* is no small step toward the solutions of your and your class's problems.

EXAMINING THE WAYS IN WHICH STUDENTS VIEW SUBJECTS

Have you ever heard an adult say, "I hate math! I was never any good at it in school, and I still can't add two and two!" or, "I never got the hang of reading. My friend can sit there and read by the hour; two minutes with a magazine and I'm bored!"? The seeds of these attitudes are sown with our first introduction to the subjects, which came from one of two primary sources: The teacher in school or those around us. The mother who comments within earshot of her child, "I hope Amy doesn't have the trouble with math that I had!" may have triggered a negative attitude which could affect Amy's development in arithmetic. So, too, the teacher who introduces new material by saying, "Now we're going to get into something which you may have some problems with . . ." may be triggering the same thing. Give a child an excuse for a poor attitude or performance, and he just may take it.

Keep two thoughts in mind: We like what we can do well, and we do well that which we know. This rules out excuses if every new thing is built on what we already know and the strengths we already possess. For then skills lead to interest in concepts; interest leads to skills in skill subjects. Consequently, the higher the interest level the more it helps developing skills which, in turn, leads to more interests. Make sure, therefore, that you are positively enthusiastic about what you present, and you will find that like a forest fire the enthusiasm spreads throughout your class. We have never met a child who has failed to learn in the hands of a dedicated, creative, and *enthusiastic* teacher.

Also, become aware of certain social prejudices which may have an effect on how a child may view his performance within a given subject area. The stereotyping goes something like this:

Everybody knows that boys do poorly in English but do well in Science, and girls are terrible in Science, but they do beautifully in English. Always be on the lookout to combat these inhibitors of education, as well as any other thing which may affect student outlooks. Surprisingly enough, one of these is time.

THE UNIQUE PLACE OF "TIME" IN EDUCATION

Who says that school has to run from 8 a.m. to 3 p.m., Monday through Friday, from the first week in September through the second or third week in June? Who says that's the best time for learning? We don't know about you, but we are rarely sane (much less awake) before ten in the morning, and some of our best work is done after eleven at night. We'd much rather stay at home when it registers twenty below zero, but we have tremendous energy and enthusiasm when it's sunny and seventy degrees. We're not saying that we are the norm, but we are saying that school, to which we have devoted our lives, does not fit *our* biological clocks. Over the years we have become convinced that it doesn't fit some student's clocks either.

As we see it, there are four major time factors which have an effect upon education. Perhaps to be aware of them will help lessen their detrimental influence upon the chances of success for you and your class. The time factors are:

1. TIME OF DAY—Certain subjects are better taught at certain times of the day. Some teachers have found that skill work is best done early in the day with concept work best done in the afternoon—others find the situation reversed. If you have the latitude, organize the time schedule of your subjects to best suit the optimum productivity levels of you and your students.

2. DAY OF THE WEEK—Some students and teachers see the week in terms of a playground slide. Monday is the climb to the top, and after that it is all down hill until Friday. Still others see the week as a swim on the ocean—fine once you get into it, but the first

plunge will nearly kill you. Again, if school policy permits, fit your most dramatic techniques into the days where there is a natural ebb of enthusiasm.

3. TIME OF YEAR—It is difficult to generalize on how people view the ten month school year. Generally, however, the first two months are investigative, the next five are developmental, and the last three seem devoted to reinforcement and projection toward the next year. Granted that this is simplistic, but it can be indicative of the optimum placement of types of work. For example, class-wide projects are rarely done in the first two months.

4. SPECIAL TIMES—There are certain times when "all bets are off." Ends of marking periods, the times just before or after major vacations, opening of various sports seasons (if the school is involved), various regional events (Mardi Gras, Winter Carnival, Rose Parade, etc.), all engender built-in excitement and have a tendency to throw a well-planned schedule completely off tilt. Wherever possible, the teacher should be aware of the problem and try to incorporate these special times into the regular class planning.

Anticipating that these time problems will arise, may well be the first step to their elimination as a cause of concern. Also, a good sense of time will help when considering the "frustration factor."

PINPOINTING AND ELIMINATING THE "FRUSTRATION FACTOR"

"Forget it, I can't do it! I don't get it! I don't understand it! It's stupid, anyway!" A book is slammed shut, feet go out from under a desk, arms are folded across a chest, and a mind is turned off. What we have just described is a child who has reached his "frustration factor."

We've seen it time and again. The frustration factor as we define it, is the point at which one or more students begin to leave us—they've had it; they just give up! Sometimes it is because of ability (as you discovered from your Skill Chart), sometimes it is poor self-image or peer acceptance (as you discovered from the Social Diagram), sometimes it is because of distracted interest (special events in *his* time clock), or it may be a combination of all of these plus hidden causes. Whatever it is, we must deal with it quickly in order to prevent a single brush with frustration from becoming a pattern of failure. With this goal, possibly the two most effective techniques for lessening the occurrence of the frustration factor are:

1. Good planning with a variety of activities, and
2. Open ended options.

Let's use an example within the framework of a class in Social Studies. You are doing a unit of the succession of the English kings. In your planning you would include a certain amount of memorized material, written data, investigative reading, discussions, film strips or movies, and perhaps even a story about some of the kings. While the children might not do phenomenally in all aspects, this would allow them to grasp the over-all material. Your discovery techniques within the unit would have options built in to understand the material on three levels of stimulus:

1. TACTILE—perhaps through a project or diorama.
2. VISUAL—reading or watching a film strip.
3. AUDIAL—class discussions and the movie.

Now you have covered all the bases. The material is covered and retained on more than one level, and each child has at least two opportunities for success instead of being locked into only one method and any inherent frustrations it may bring.

Careful planning and multiple options are needed to reduce the frustration factor and create opportunities for a breakthrough in thinking.

THE BREAKTHROUGH—
THE SIGNAL OF CHANGE

Discovery techniques are used for many reasons. We must always make certain, however, that the technique used is appropriate. That was the main reason why you filled out the

Social Diagram and the Skill Chart—to make certain you were doing precisely what the class and/or the individual needed in the way of reinforcement and development. If you have used a technique to spur interest, and it has worked, then that breakthrough is a signal to you that it is time to change techniques to keep in line with the development of the child.

If, for example, you are trying to interest a child in something, and he indeed becomes interested, then we must try to keep that interest by changing to techniques that will take the child further along. Or, if we have been trying to keep a student interested in one subject, and he begins exploring other contingent subjects, that is another change for which we must be prepared.

A teacher wants to interest Alan in learning spelling words, and she succeeds so well that Alan wants to begin writing compositions using them. Not to switch to techniques for helping Alan develop his writing skills at this point, would be to miss a fantastic opportunity to aid in the child's discovery of his writing potential.

Consequently, you should keep your discovery techniques structured. They should fall into the following categories:

1. BASIC—Techniques aimed at getting initial interest, getting over the hump of a minor frustration factor, or the introduction of new material.
2. INTERMEDIATE—Keeping the interest generated and adding new skills to promote development.
3. ADVANCED—Techniques with high interest and needed skills which motivate the student to explore on his own.

Structure techniques in this way, and you can't miss. You know where you are going, you know what is needed, and by careful selection of your discovery techniques, you know how to get there.

"WHY, GEORGE, I THINK YOU'VE GOT IT"

We'd like to share with you an actual experience with a child whom we shall call George:

"George was the perfect example of a kid who could not sit and listen to something and have it make sense. The lesson was on verb endings. The rules were explained over and over again by the teacher, but past, present and future was all the same to George. The frustration factor of George and his teacher was reaching an all time high. Finally, it was the teacher who asked for help.

"I got a basketball from the gym and gave it to George. I asked him, 'What do you think will happen if it drops?' 'It'll bounce,' he said, looking at me as if I were a simpleton. 'O.K.,' I said, 'do it.' He did. 'What's it doing?' I asked. 'Bouncing,' he replied. I grabbed the ball from him. 'When you dropped it before, what did it do?' 'What else,' George replied, 'it bounced!' "Now who says you don't understand verb tense; you just used it.' 'I did not, I was playin' with a basketball!' 'Were you?' I said. I led him to my desk . . . "

The point of this anecdote is that George could, indeed, learn verb tense, in fact he became quite good at it. However, he, and many other students like him, could not learn *only* by listening. Even having him put words on a blackboard would not have made it real for George. George had to *see* and *touch* as well as hear in order for him to understand.

Remember that we may have a child like George in our classroom. Try to use techniques that involve as many of the senses as possible. The individual who needs that kind of instruction will benefit from it, and so will our entire class.

Chapter 7

Guidelines
for Discovery
in Key Subject Areas

One of the joys of education, for us at least, is watching an enthusiastic, creative teacher at work with a class. Over the years it has been our privilege to meet and know many such educators. Their techniques for instilling a sense of discovery in their students are outstanding and, needless to say, practical and tested under a variety of conditions. It is an honor to be able to share some of them with you.

EXAMINING KEY FACTORS IN DEVELOPING SKILLS

Let us start with the understanding that some drill work *is* necessary. There is no way around it. Given a particular method of reading, students *must* learn basic sounds, ph-, gh-, cl-, sh-, etc., or, for math the multiplication tables are a must. Call it rote, call it drill, call it repetition, call it what you will, there are certain skills which must be taught again and again until the student internalizes them and does them automatically. After all, we know many adults who have paid good money to have a thousand tennis balls shot at them until their backhand becomes automatic.

To say that this must cut down on creativity is simply not true. Of course we must do drill work, but it is within our power to make it interesting, exciting, and part of the discovery process. Be aware that our own reluctance to teach something can be passed on, albeit subtly, to our students. Keep *your* enthusiasm for these subjects high, particularly at the point of drill work, and it will carry over to your class.

One thing that will help you is explaining or showing your students the need for the skill. "I'm going to show you a way you can help your parents when you go to the store with them," says one teacher we know when she begins the multiplication tables. For the vast majority of the class, this is sufficient. Five oranges at ten cents each comes to fifty cents as the students are soon telling their parents at the local supermarket.

Another teacher writes a story on the level of the students, but she leaves out all punctuation and capitalization. Then she has various students try to read it to the class. The results are often funny, and everybody laughs. It is also a tremendous and perfectly natural lead-in to the study of punctuation.

Another device that helps with skill work is the clever use of mnemonic devices. We can tell you the colors of the spectrum in their natural order, because when we were small a teacher told us about the little man who was the keeper of the spectrum. His name was Roy G. Biv. Too many years have passed since that class, yet we still remember that character and what his name stood for: *R*ed, *O*range, *Y*ellow, *G*reen, *B*lue, *I*ndigo, *V*iolet.

Children across the nation still sing the alphabet song, Tommy Thumb and Peter Pointer still teach the names of the fingers, and whenever we type "Mississippi" our minds can't help but sing "M-I-S, S-I-S, S-I-P-P-I!" Mnemonics are fascinating, they're fun, and *they are remembered.*

In helping your class develop skills keep in mind that drill work is a necessary and vital part of the curriculum. Remember also that far from being boring or dull, it can be made practical and fun through your personal enthusiasm and creativity.

UTILIZING DISCOVERY TECHNIQUES
IN LANGUAGE ARTS

Language Arts is, possibly, the single most necessary subject our students will ever learn. Reading, writing and speaking are universal needs in a civilized world. The child who cannot read is *lost,* not just in school, but in life as well. Without a foundation in language arts skills the child is not going to succeed in math, will not comprehend his science classes, and will do no research in social studies nor do well in any of his subjects since all of education is based on the understanding of and facility with the reading, writing and speech tools of language arts.

Throughout the first six chapters of this book we have tried to stress the fact that discovery techniques are purposeful—that is, they are pinpointed and tailor-made for particular individuals and classes in specific situations. This need for precision is particularly apparent in the field of language arts. If, out of a class of twenty-five students, three kids don't remember who succeeded Henry VII as King of England, it will not prove tremendously detrimental to them twenty years from now. If, however, out of that same class of twenty five there is even one student who does not know how to read, that will be detrimental, twenty hours, twenty months, and twenty years from now.

Through the use of the Skill Chart and the Skill Chart Diagram (Figures 6-3 and 6-4) you were able to determine problem areas within your class. Use these in determining the thrust of discovery techniques in the skill subjects. Aim part of them at the entire class, more of them at small groups, and the majority of them at individuals and individual needs. Realize that through language arts we are preparing the student for survival in every other area of his life. Language arts is the skeleton upon which is fashioned the muscle and flesh of a complete education. Take that extra time, work with the individual, and make certain that that foundation is solid.

CHECKLIST OF INDIVIDUAL AND CLASSWIDE DISCOVERY TECHNIQUES IN SPELLING

A teacher who has served many years in the classroom offers this classwide technique for spelling with which she has had great success:

UP IN THE AIR—Each new word is introduced separately. It is written on the blackboard by the teacher in syllables.

The children look at the word, say the word, and then use
their index fingers to write the word in the air. Any
difficulties with the word (trick endings, etc.) are
explained by the teacher. The children then look at it, say
it again, and close their eyes and write it again in the air,
this time spelling it out loud.

You might also try:

LETTER MIX—A day or so after the words have been
introduced, the class is given a mimeographed sheet with
the spelling words scrambled. Their task is to unscramble
each word and write it correctly. It is great fun for the
students, reinforces the spelling words, and since several
words from previous spelling lessons were always included,
it kept students on their toes.

There are variations on this latter technique. For a slower
group you might have the first or last two letters in correct
order and the students have to rearrange either end, or for a
rather advanced group, present all the letters used in the words
in an unbroken chain (aaaa, bb, ccccc, d, ee, etc.) and allow
them to determine the words from there.

For group work, consider using:

CONSPICUOUS CAPITALS—Have the students write the
spelling words, placing those parts of the words with which
they are most likely to have trouble in capitals. For
example, if a spelling word were "arrangement," the parts
most likely to cause difficulty are the double r and the ge.
Therefore, the students would write the word—aRRanGE-
ment. You can help, of course, but this is most effective if
the students themselves determine what parts of a word
will cause them the problems.

For individual reinforcement, these have proven effective:

WORD PLAY—Difficult spelling words may become somewhat easier if colorful mnemonic devices are used. "A

superintendENT collects the rENT," "Bury your E's in the cEmEtEry," and "The princiPAL is your PAL" are just a few. There are many books which contain such helps, or better yet, have the individual student make up his own.

Also, since learning is a total process you might try:

TOUCH AND SPELL—A shallow box covered with loose sand is used. The student spells the word in the sand, using his *entire hand and arm* and saying the syllables as he writes. Have the student do this several times, then write the word on paper, saying it each time. This makes the word a part of the physical child as well as something in his mind. Substitutes might be used, such as a large sheet of drawing paper and a liquid marker held at arm's length, but from experience, the sand works best.

Moreover, do not neglect such time-honored techniques as compositions using the spelling words, spelling "bees," and the many fine spelling games using letter cubes and tiles that are currently available in stores. Each has its place in developing spelling skills.

THE RELUCTANT "R"—READING

Sometimes early skill work seems like a separate entity from the words and stories that the children are learning. Here are two techniques devised by Mrs. Barbara A. Dean, a reading teacher, to relate skills and phonics to any word the children could possibly meet:

BE THE TEACHER—"In the beginning of the year, one of the things you go over are long and short vowel sounds. It is hard for a first or second grader to see the difference between R-O-B-E with a long O and R-O-B, no E, pronounced with a short O. The garment you put around you and the act of stealing it are remarkably alike, at least in words. Once the skills have been learned, 'E at the end makes the vowel long but itself silent,' and 'The vowel is short if it has no E or Y to help it,' the children must have ways of using them. A very effective technique is for the teacher and the students to switch roles. The teacher reads a passage from the student's book, purposely mispronouncing vowels. The children become delighted as they 'help her' over each error. The teacher's cries of, 'But I'm sure that's right!' and 'But why isn't it right?' are met not only with repetition of skills, but then with explanations that show how well the children are internalizing."

The second technique grew out of the frustration that Mrs. Dean experienced when she taught a skill which the children understood when they had words they recognized, but would say, "I can't read that word; I never saw it before."

SOMETHING IN NOTHING—"I drew up a group of nonsense words at the end of each skill I taught. At first, even three-letter words like GUB caused the class to stumble. But, as their skills developed, they knew what the word had to sound like, for they knew the sound of G, short U, and B. A little later on, they met words like GINE, FETTY, BAV, AND PIM. The fertile imagination of the children made up clever definitions of each word, and they could pronounce them properly using their skills. The beginning reader is faced with a whole world of nonsense words (at least to him), but by showing him that his skills can unlock *any* word, he has found a purpose.

"One other thought on this: It has always been known that the child's speaking vocabulary is larger than his reading vocabularly which is, in turn, larger than his spelling vocabulary. By using this technique in the middle grades, children gained the added reinforcement of bringing all their skills a little closer to each other. For example, I purposely misspelled EQUINOX after pronouncing it for my class by putting a Z at the end. I was met with a young man's protest that there had to be an X at the end, because that was what it sounded like. To use skills is to retain them."

In encouraging the reluctant 'R' keep in mind that constant repetition of skills, vocal reinforcement, and sometimes techniques that incorporate surprises, are all effective tools for use.

YOUR GUIDE TO STUDENT USE
OF MATH SKILLS

Math is a difficult subject to teach. It requires that the teacher explain not only the concepts, but that the children are given ample and meaningful opportunities to use them. It stands to reason, therefore, that the more exciting and relevant the technique, the greater the discovery on the part of the students and the greater the retention as well. The following technique was devised by Mrs. Marian R. Kittell for use with city children to aid in teaching the age old problem of units, tens, and hundreds. It is called:

APARTMENT HOUSE—The technique begins with a story and a simple drawing on the blackboard which the children can copy and keep at their desks. The story goes like this: "There was this apartment house. It only had room for single people. They don't have a family. Sometimes they share rooms, but they're still just singles. There are many floors in the apartment house, but there are only single people living on all of them. Next door, there is another apartment house. It's much bigger—in fact, ten times bigger. In it live families, and the rooms are so designed that for people to move in there, there must be ten in the family. Aunts and uncles, brothers and sisters, cats and dogs, can all live in here, as long as there are only ten of them. This apartment house, too, has many floors. Sometimes the families grow soooooo big that they have to move into the gigantic apartment house next door. It's for all the friends and relatives to live together." It is obvious that what is being introduced is the concept of units, tens, and hundreds. The progression may be carried further by saying something like, "They move into a development full of houses (thousands)" or "They inhabit a town (ten thousands)." The drawing of each apartment house indicates ten floors. The teacher continues the lesson by problems such as, "Billy's family has 123 people in it. How many can live in the big apartment house, the middle size, and the small one?" In such a way, units, tens, hundreds become visual and meaningful to the children.

The drawing that accompanies this is just an outline of a block with some floors, with the one to the left being half again as big as the one to the right.

Quite often, teachers come up against the problem, particularly in the primary grades, of the student who has memorized the fact that $1 + 4 = 5$, but is completely thrown when the problem is stated $4 + 1 = ?$ Perhaps this technique will aid in such cases:

THE SWITCH—Some children have to have tactile and visual reinforcement of skills in order to retain them. In this case the teacher has a large shoebox filled with bottle caps. It might also be milk caps, poker chips, or bingo markers, but they should be heavy enough so they will not move if a child breathes on them or moves a desk. By weight, pennies are ideal, but they disappear. Also needed is construction paper. The easiest to come by are the ones no one else wants like purple, pink, and off green. Don't use good colors for this, since it is only used as background for the caps. The children keep the paper at their desks, and the caps are returned to the shoebox.

When the teacher hands out the paper, she draws a line down the center (For upper primary there could be more than one division.). Now the teacher continues, "I have four apples (placing four on the board) and four apple cores (placing four on the board next to the first but across the line). How many apples did I have?" The children place four markers to the left of the line and four markers to the right. By counting all the markers, they know that there were eight apples to start. For subtraction, the children are told that there were eight apples.

They place eight markers on one side of the line. They are told that four were eaten, and they move four to the other side. By counting the number left, they arrive at the answer, four.

Especially with children who know, for instance, that one plus four equals five but stumble when asked what four plus one equals, drill with the bottlecaps combining teacher explanation and guidance with the tactile manipulation of the juxtaposition of actual objects might go a long way toward solving the problem.

Middle grades like to work with money. One teacher incorporated the skills of addition, subtraction, multiplication, division, decimals and fractions all into a unit on money.

SHOPPER'S PARADISE—For a certain period of time (in this case four weeks) the children received paper play money and disks for tasks done in the classroom. At the end of the third week, they were given opportunities to "buy" items from a catalog they had made up from magazines. For example, one group of four children got ten "dollars" for handing in a group project. They had to figure out how much each one had made. They did one-fourth of the work, so they received one-fourth of the money.

When it came time to make the "purchases," the children had to subtract each one of the items from the total money available. Since there were no refunds and all sales were final, a great deal of figuring was done. Heretofore complicated and intangible concepts such as interest, shipping and handling costs, and depreciation suddenly became real as these little shoppers tried to get the most for their money.

These techniques are practical, they use materials at hand, and they are excitingly effective. Let's look at more techniques in other fields.

HOW TO INSURE SUCCESS
IN ART AND MUSIC

THE SPANGLED PANDEMONIUM

by

Palmer Brown

The Spangled Pandemonium
Is missing from the zoo.
He bent the bars the barest bit,
And slithered glibly through.
He crawled across the moated wall.
He climbed the mango tree,
And when his keeper scrambled up,
He nipped him in the knee.
To all of you, a warning,
Not to wander after dark.
Or if you must, make very sure
You stay out of the park.
For the Spangled Pandemonium
Is missing from the zoo.
And since he nipped his keeper,
He would just as soon nip you![1]

This delightful poem was used by Judith L. Sorkowitz, a very creative and innovative art teacher, to increase her student's use of imagination, originality and descriptive additions in drawing. The technique is called:

MENTAL IMAGES—It is explained that "mental images" are the pictures that you get inside your head when you hear something, and that you can't help but get them. The children are instructed to pay particular attention to their mental images while the teacher reads them something. The poem is now read to the class. Then they discuss where it took place. Then the teacher goes back and points

[1] "The Spangled Pandemonium" from BEYOND THE PAWPAW TREES, by Palmer Brown. Reprinted by permission of Harper & Row, Publishers, Inc.

out all the descriptive words that might lead the children to see what the Spangled Pandemonium looked like. Words like "slithered," "crawled," "climbed," "nipped," and facts like he bent the bars, he lived in a zoo, and he went to the park lead to speculations like, "Why did he leave the zoo?" "Why did he bite his keeper?" and "What happens if you go out after dark?" The children become involved in this as they call out possible answers. Then each child is given paper and told to draw the Spangled Pandemonium with the teacher saying, "I don't know what it looks like, can you help me?" or "The zoo keeper will probably ask the policeman to catch the Spangled Pandemonium. Let's give the policeman a picture to help him."

Any piece of writing can be taken through these steps, if like "The Spangled Pandemonium" by Palmer Brown, it does not tell you anything at all about what the subject looks like, but rather leaves it to the imagination.

Certain techniques have certain optimum ages. This one is right on target in late fifth and early sixth grades. Skill development is good, and imagination is untethered. A piece of oaktag, stiff construction paper, or light cardboard can be the basic ingredient in this technique called:

MOBILE FACES—Children cut out the shape of a face from the center of the paper. Then, within the center of this face, they draw and cut out eyes, nose, mouth, moustache, eyebrows, etc. They color both sides of the parts of the face, but not necessarily the same way. For example, the moustache can be black on one side and red on the other. Colored pieces of string are connected to the pieces with tape, or a dab of glue may be used. The pieces are then hung within the opening of the face where they would belong. (This is done by shortening strings. The eyebrows would have a shorter string than the eyes.) The pieces swing freely in the face opening and also show both sides. Spatial relationships and facial anatomy are but two of the reinforced skills shown by this technique.

Finally, here's a device to spur imagination through the use of something that is already begun. It's called:

I AM WHAT I AM—The teacher cuts lengths of yarn and has the students sit at their desks with a piece of paper in front of them. The teacher drops a piece of yarn on to the paper, and the student, without moving it and leaving it just where it fell, must construct a picture around it. At first glance, the technique seems simple and without purpose, but here is a technique that has the student structuring his creativity. By the time a child is in seventh grade, he can draw for hours. Here is an opportunity for him to draw anything he wants except that it must conform at some point to the configuration of the yarn.

Most of the teachers we have spoken to have all stressed the need for basic, fundamental skills. In the area of music, too, children must acquire a basic background in order to develop a sense of music appreciation, notes and time values, and the joy of making pleasant, recognizable sounds. Mr. Secondo Neri has developed two delightful techniques for teaching the notes of the scale and what can be done with them for primary and middle-grade students. The first one he calls:

GIVING NOTES AWAY—Mr. Neri begins the class by passing out pieces of paper. On each piece there is either the letter of the note, the name of the tone (do, re, me, etc.), or the type of note (whole note, half, quarter). As he passes out the last pieces of paper, he begins to look worried. As the last piece of paper leaves his hands, he goes to his desk and, looking dejected, lowers his head. One of the children usually asks what is wrong. "I was going to teach you the notes today," he answers, still looking sad. "Say, maybe you can help me! Does anyone have C?" Because they are passed out randomly, several children have C and at least two children have C and DO on their papers. "I have C!" one child calls out. "Great, then he can come home," Neri says as he places that note on the board in its correct position on the musical bar, "Does anybody know what he sounds like?" "He says DO!" yells the child with that on his paper. This progresses through the scale with the letter and sound name of each note as the children "help" each note to come home. Next, each child has or is given a playable musical instrument (xylophone, flutophone, or several children can share a glockenspiel or piano). Now the notes are called out, and the children who have the notes on their paper play them. For example, he would call out E, D, C, D,E, E, E. The children holding the notes E, D, and C, would then play them, discovering that they had just played the first seven notes of "Mary Had A Little Lamb." The students are learning the real names and the real positions of the notes.

His second technique is for middle grades who already have a sense of these preliminaries. He calls it:

HOW ARE YOU SOUNDING TODAY—He divides the class into groups of eight, designating each child to be a note. If there are students left over, they record the arrangement of the notes. First, the eight stand in order, and he "plays" them on an instrument. Now he turns his back and the students scramble, mixing the order. He turns back and "plays" this new "tune." Students vie to arrange themselves into new patterns, each of which is played. Eventually, they begin to discover that they need more than one of some notes to make some tunes (You can't play "Mary Had A Little Lamb" with only one E.). They begin "borrowing" children/notes from other groups. In its very basic form, they are discovering the fundamentals of composition and arrangement. We have seen this done in a choral program with great success.

When thinking of music in your classroom, do not overlook such common tunes as commercial jingles or even the top 40. Even the little ones can sing songs they hear four and five times a day. Finally, don't overlook the classics. Bring the stories of operas and ballets into the children's frame of reference and your students will not only remember them, but listen raptly as their imaginations take them on trips with Sinbad (Rimsky-

Korsakov's *Scheherazade*), they'll cry for the swan (Tchaikovsky's *Swan Lake*), or tremble in the halls of the Mountain King (Grieg's *Peer Gynt Suite*).

Moreover, don't neglect the possibilities of using music and art as the stimulus for activities in language arts, social studies, research projects, and anything else you can think of.

". . . 'I' BEFORE 'E,' EXCEPT AFTER 'C'—SOMETIMES . . . "

We do not suggest that the techniques used in the following story should be tried by everybody, for, in order to be effective, they must suit the personality of the teacher and the rapport that has been established by the teacher with the class.

"The trouble with spelling rules is that there are always exceptions. The 'I before E' rule, for example, works perfectly, except when you want to r*EI*nforce sc*IE*nce. GHOTI spells 'fish'—GH as in 'cou*gh*' = F; O as in 'w*o*men' = I; TI as in 'na*ti*on' = SH; ergo, GHOTI = fish. And, what sound does OUGH have? Consider ROUGH, BOUGH, THROUGH, and COUGH. If it's confusing to you, imagine what it must be like to a kid. I was constantly seeking for some way to get my students to remember the spelling rules *and* the exceptions.

"One child in my room was having particular difficulty with a spelling rule. One day he brought a paper to my desk with every word spelled correctly incorporating the difficult rule. I started to rise to put my arm around him when I lost my balance and fell! From the floor I shouted, "You got it! Bob, you're tremendous; you just knock me off my feet!" The class and I broke into hysterical laughter.

"Several days later, I overheard one of my students explaining a spelling rule to a student from another class. The other student remarked about how he could never remember it. My student answered, 'It's easy. That's the rule we had the day Mr. Daniels fell out of his chair!'

"That started me thinking. Perhaps a 'trigger' of some kind, be it dramatic or ludicrous, would help a child remember what is taught.

"Now, if a child rearranges letters in a word, I not only circle it, but I turn it into a funny face. I pile my desk with books and loudly knock them off to demonstrate subtraction. Once, I even stood on top of my desk to be a letter that was 'taller' when teaching capitalization. I don't use these methods all the time, but there is always that occasion which calls for the special. Whenever a block happens, and the students just can't seem to get it, they and their crazy teacher can always manage to laugh their way out of it. At the same time, however, it becomes so vivid in their minds that it is a learning experience that they will always carry with them."

Chapter 8

Applying
Discovery Techniques in
"Concept" Subjects

Once in a department store we overheard a distraught mother shout at her child, "When will you learn to think?" Upon reflection, that was not as outrageous a question as it might appear. Children in school learn many skills, but are they learning *the greatest skill*—to think? What are we, as educators, doing to teach our students to *think* in a clear, concise, and constructive manner? In this chapter, let's explore some of the ways in which this may be effectively accomplished.

HOW TO JUDGE GROWTH
IN UNDERSTANDING

Recently, we came up against a very precocious four-and-a-half year old who proceeded to recite, with a beaming parent in the background, the multiplication tables for the numbers one through six. Dutifully impressed, we got down the bowl of lollypops we keep on our bookshelf and, calling the lad to us, said, "We'd like to give you two lollypops. We'd also like to send two lollypops home with you for your brother and sister. Let's see, two lollypops each for three people. How many should we take out of the bowl?" The boy looked at his mother, at us, and at the lollypops. "I dun'no," he said, "how

121

many?" "Why don't you do your two times table," we prompted. He did. "Now," we continued, "two lollypops times three people means how many lollypops?" With large brown eyes he looked up at us, smiled, and said, "A hundred???"

The point of this anecdote is that merely because a person has memorized something—a list, chart, table, dates, etc.—it does *not* necessarily follow that the person *understands* what he has memorized. "Learning" implies conceptualization, that is, complete internalization of the given material, and the ability to relate that material to other situations. That the boy could recite the multiplication tables showed his ability to memorize, but unless he can internalize those facts and use them to determine, for example, precisely how many lollypops must be taken from the bowl, he does not understand, and he has not learned.

When developing conceptualizations, make certain that emphasis is not as much on the rightness or wrongness of answers but on how they have arrived at the answer in the first place. Start that process early. There is no reason why a first grader can't be expected to give a reason for an answer. The reason may be totally wrong, but you have at least required that he *thought through* the process. If a child can figure out why he got something wrong, not only will he never get it wrong again, but he has learned as much as the child who got the answer right. Furthermore, if the process of sequential/relative thinking is begun early enough, that process develops along with the child till it produces a functioning, thinking adult. If a child is old enough to learn the skill, he can also conceptualize it.

Along with actual curricular material, give opportunities to test judgments and thinking skills. One of the most popular activities we have tried with classes on all levels is a sheet generally titled "Can You Follow Directions?" It consists of some twenty or thirty written directions which the class is told they must follow in order to "pass." The first direction usually reads, "Please read everything on this paper before you do anything else." The second statement reads, "Sign your name on the top of this paper." Then follow many directions requiring the students to do anything from drawing a funny face on th back of the paper to getting up and running three times around their desks. The last direction on the paper, however, states, "Now that you have read everything as you were directed in number one, all you have to do to pass is answer direction number two."[1]

Many times it is hilarious to watch. The vast majority of students go through the whole list one at a time until they come to that final direction. Then, when the light dawns upon them, what groans and moans! Everyone has a good laugh, but they have learned something as well. If you decide to try this, better make up a number of extras—they all want to take one home to try out on their parents.

This technique, while extremely entertaining and productive, is aimed at teaching thinking separately. Now let's look at ways in which the thinking skills may be developed in the concept subjects of history, social studies, and science.

DEVELOPING NEW APPROACHES TO HISTORY AND SOCIAL STUDIES

It is obvious that the teacher determines the point of view that the students will take within a given subject. If, for example, the teacher is battle/name/date-oriented, that is what the class will get, and that will be their approach to the subject. We'll be honest, it's much easier to teach that way. Either they know the date of the battle and the names of the generals, or they don't. If they do, they pass; if they don't, they fail. It's quick, it's simple, and there is definitely no *thought* required.

Thankfully, we know of no teachers who are subjecting their classes to this method. Indeed, educators realize that the understanding of why, how, and what happened will be remembered long after the date of the battle has faded from memory.

If you will grant us that the most important thing for your classes to get from their "concept" subjects is a facility of mind, then you will keep adding information that they will build with

---

[1]See Karlin and Berger, *Successful Methods for Teaching the Slow Learner,* Parker Publishing Co., West Nyack, N.Y. 1969.

later. You will never give a piece of data whose only purpose is to be parroted back on a test but otherwise never used.

Did you know that the average rainfall in the Republic of Chad is five inches per year? Isn't that interesting? Frankly, we can't get too excited about it. However, relate that fact to the difficulties of farming and the consequent nomadic nature of the inhabitants and even how this affects problems of government, and now it does become important, and we can find it exciting and interesting.

There are three ways in which we can insure that our students are getting the most out of any concept subject. They are:

I. PROPER INTRODUCTION—Before starting something, check the skill requirements. Go over needed vocabulary, pertinant facts that they may be using, and even research skills if needed.

"We're going to continue with the story of the Revolution. Here's a sheet with some new words that we'll be meeting. (Here the teacher passes out the papers and pronounces the words.) I'd like you to look them up in the dictionary. Also, we'll need some facts to continue with the Revolution, and I have them listed here. (Teacher hands out paper.) We'll be using both these sheets, and we'll be going to the library. Does anyone know the best way to look up a book? The first name on this list is Nathan Hale. Suppose I wanted a book about him; how would I go about it?"

This introduction which takes between five and twenty minutes, serves three purposes: The children are provided with the tools they need to start; they have begun a definite, structured procedure which will lead them into the subject; and their curiosity has been teased and motivation begun.

II. PROPER METHOD—Allow opportunities for the class to discover causes for events by giving background rather than known or easily found information. Reading the textbook should be resource work, not the backbone of learning. It is here, particularly, that the teacher's knowledge and creativity can best serve the class.

Here is what one teacher did during a lesson on the ride of Paul Revere: "The Sons of Liberty had a problem. They had to figure out a way to get a message past the British. Hand carrying a letter was dangerous and it was too slow. Furthermore, the British were going to move at night. The best way to give a signal at night seemed to be a light. But where would they put it? Most of the buildings in Boston at that time were only one or two stories tall. That wasn't high enough to be seen very far. Then someone mentioned the Old North Church. It was the tallest building in town and the belfry could hold a man with a light . . . "

The idea of the problems of the time, the structures of the buildings, and why Old North Church was so ideal, gives students a background and feeling of the time they might otherwise miss. Proper questioning would further involve the students.

III. PROPER REVIEW—Pose questions in such a way that the students will have to *think* in order to get the answer rather than just testing memory.

Here are two questions:

What was Paul Revere's signal from Old North Church?

How did Paul Revere spread the news?

Now here are questions which test the same knowledge, but they are geared to requiring thought:

What did the size and location of Old North Church have to do with Paul Revere?

Why did Paul Revere use a horse instead of a horse and wagon?

While we have applied these three techniques to history, there is no reason why they may not be equally applied to geography, literature, science, or any other concept subject.

PRACTICAL METHODS OF DISCOVERY IN SCIENCE

We have visited schools where the science classes have enough microscopes for every child in the room to have his own with which to work. We have also seen schools where the science teacher is lucky to have a demonstration table, let alone equipment for experiments. Before any science lesson is begun, therefore, it is a good idea to check what materials you have available in the light of what you wish to teach. Nothing is so frustrating to both teacher and students than to progress to a certain point only to find out that they can't continue because of lack of a certain piece of equipment. Here, the Discovery Potential Guide should prove of great value to you.

The Discovery Potential Guide will also be an aid to you in determining whether your students can actually handle what you had in mind. Also, a look at the Skill Chart will show you if they have the tools with which to understand. The Social Diagram will tell you if your class can work in groups, be left alone with equipment, or needs constant supervision. If, for example, these forms have shown you that your class has difficulty tying their shoelaces, contains ten kids with overtly aggressive behavior patterns, and the kids have to be hand led to the lavatory so they can find their way back, we would suggest *you* cut up the frog and let them watch rather than placing scalpels in their hands!

In science, particularly, work must be done on multiple (sequential) directions. The scientific method, of its very nature, teaches logic. One thing must follow another in order to arrive at a solution. The teacher must make every effort to insure that students understand this concept.

A third grade teacher taught this sense of sequence through a method she called:

> BUILDING BODIES WITH MIKE—The teacher had an anatomical dummy (available from any scientific supply house) which came apart. Instead of using the dummy merely to illustrate and name the various parts (lungs, heart, blood vessels, etc.), her class arrived one day to find the dummy completely taken apart and the various pieces strewn in profusion on a work table. "That's my friend, Mike," the teacher told the students, "and you've all seen Mike on the shelf. Today, I want you to put Mike together." Without any help from her, the students set about the task. Eventually, Mike got together. In the process, the students learned many things. For instance,

they found out that the heart was behind the lungs, the kidneys were in back, and the stomach went underneath the diaphragm. Of course, they didn't know all the names yet, and it was a giant jigsaw puzzle. By the end of the unit, however, they were putting Mike back together while naming each part. They now did it in seconds.

Did the technique work? To answer that question you had to be present to hear a little third grade girl tell us, "I gotta go now. It's my turn, and I gotta put in Mike's eustacian tube."

Obviously, the apparatus involved is not that important. What does matter is the teacher's approach to the subject. It might have been constructing a phylum tree, making an airplane, or modeling a volcano. The teacher allowed her students to discover, and then she led them, step by step, to a natural conclusion based on their own discoveries. That third grade girl not only knew what a eustacian tube was, but where it was located in her body, and why her ears popped when she had a cold.

Finally, do not neglect a student's natural curiosity as a starting point for learning. If a student comes to you with a legitimate question, "Why do my papers blow off my desk only when the window *and* the door are open?" then use that question. If you're teaching air currents or weather, it's perfect, and you can use it class wide. If not, pose the question to the entire class, direct the student who posed the question to the sources where he may find the answer, and have that student report his findings to the class. In this way, everyone has benefited. Moreover, no student will ever hesitate to ask a question in this type of atmosphere for fear that it will be considered "dumb."

HOW TO AVOID CONFUSION WHEN USING A MULTI-DISCIPLINE APPROACH

All that "Multi-Discipline Approach" means is the correlation of more than one subject within a unit of study. This process has many names, but the basic pattern remains the same. For example, suppose a unit on China were being taught. Under a Multi-Discipline Approach, instead of learning about China only in their history class, students would read stories about China in their reading class, learn monetary systems and the use of the abacus in their math class, study some Chinese inventions in science, learn about Chinese painting in art, and perhaps even hear some a-tonal music in that class. Hopefully, when the unit is completed, the student comes away *not* with a one-sided textbook view, but a fully developed concept of what is China.

Before you decide that the Multi-Discipline Approach is for you, and you want to start it with your classes tomorrow, let us suggest that it is not without its problems. Depending upon whether your class is homogeneous, heterogeneous, departmentalized, or self-contained there are attendant problems which, while far from insurmountable, you should be aware of before you try anything of this nature.

With a *homogeneously grouped* class, the problems lie in the *level* of teaching. We cannot present our class with material they are not equipped to handle. The homogeneous class may be on a high, median, or low level of ability. Consequently, gear materials to the level of *their* understanding. A reference to the Skill Chart you made out earlier will be helpful in pinpointing what your class can handle.

In a *heterogeneously grouped* class, the problems lie within the *method* of teaching. It is obvious that within such a class there are many different ability levels, and students will be learning at different rates. Therefore, methods must expand to become all-inclusive. The same material must be covered from a variety of angles in order that it may reach not only the student who will pick it up at once but also the student who may need multi-sensory contacts before he can assimilate and conceptualize.

If you work in a *departmentalized* setup, your problems quite often come from *personalities.* Not, as you might imagine, from those of the students, but from those of the faculty members engaged in the Multi-Disciplinary Approach. Questions such as who will introduce the unit, how much and what is to be taught by each teacher, in what order will it be taught, what will be the criteria for evaluation, what and how much homework will be given, and how will it satisfy the curriculum requirements for each department, must all be answered *before* anything is begun. If five departments are in a unit, you may find yourself faced with five different answers to each question. Such variables as teaching styles and methods, class management philosophies, and personal ability to compromise, must all be considered. Perhaps the easiest way to overcome these difficulties is to begin with one other teacher with whom you can work and then begin to expand, based upon your successes.

In a *self-contained* classroom, the problem is *time*. First, there are certain things which *must* be done, skill work for example must be done every day, there are minor interruptions with which to cope, requirements from the main office which must be met, etc. Consequently, the Multi-Disciplinary Approach must be structured to incorporate the real, every day necessities of the classroom. Second, understand that students may get caught up in one aspect of the approach to the exclusions of others. It is our task to keep the class's perspective in line. And finally, the student's sense of certain times for certain subjects may become altered. Reading may not be taught in the morning as it has since September if the class is engaged upon a particular project that requires their attention then and there. It is because of this lack of set routine that we do not suggest using this approach below third grade.

If you have read this far and decided that you will *never* use this approach, let us suggest that there are some very definite benefits to be gained by it. The major benefit is that students gain a sense of proportion and totality. Granted that the world is made up of pieces, but they are inter-related to form a whole. A Multi-Disciplinary Approach gives students just this sense of the *gestalt*. Next, students gain a sense of relevance. What they are taught in one class has a direct bearing on what they learn in another class. And, finally, the student does not receive merely a compendium of facts, but a feeling of the clockwork aspects of life with all its nuances inter-relating.

HOW TO EXPAND CONCEPTS
TO ALLOW STUDENT THEORIZING

Let's come out of the ivory tower of "shoulds" and get into how the theories can help *your* class. We'll take one sample lesson, show you the plans, the questions, the materials, how to involve all types of stimuli, how to add the unique to spur memory, and when not to give an answer. The final section of this chapter will show you how a presentation of the material can give the student a sense of being there.

Our sample lesson will be on the Battle of Gettysburg. It is taken from a unit on the Civil War.

The materials needed for the lesson are a map of the area, a piece of woolen clothing, a piece of cotton clothing, a cardboard box containing four bricks, a coffee can filled with small stones, blackboard, chalk, an electric room heater, and pages 136-141 of the textbook.

The questions to be answered are:

Why did Lee leave the mountains and go into the Pennsylvania farmlands?

What were the physical advantages of "Billy Yank" over "Johnny Reb?"

What were the advantages of "Johnny Reb" over "Billy Yank?"

Did the generals have a choice about where they fought?

What did a pair of shoes have to do with the Battle of Gettysburg?

The plan for the lesson is simple: To make the students see, feel, and experience the Battle of Gettysburg from both sides.

Before we begin the actual lesson let us point out several facts. First, the materials required are rather unique, and they are not commonly found in a classroom. You will find that their uses will also be unique. The questions are not only intriguing; they are the kind that cannot be answered by a name, date, or one-line fact from a textbook.

Ready for the lesson? O.K., let's begin.

A PAIR OF SHOES

As the students enter the room they find the windows closed, and as the last one is seated, the teacher closes the door and turns on an electric room heater. Without any comment by the teacher, the class begins.

"Before we begin today's lesson," the teacher says, "can anyone tell us where General Lee was and what he was doing when we last saw him?"

Several students volunteer answers.

The teacher turns to the blackboard and, toward the bottom, draws the peaks of the mountains where the students have told her Lee was. As she turns back, she notices some buzzing in the room.

"What is it? What's going on?"

"Can we open a window?" one child asks, "It's getting hot in here with that heater on."

"You'll get used to it," the teacher answers. "Now who remembers where General Grant was?"

Fewer students volunteer this information. The room is becoming perceptably warmer.

"I want a drink of water," one child shouts.

"So do I, but we don't have any in the room. By the way, I need a volunteer. Who's the strongest person in this class?"

Urged by several classmates, one boy rises to his feet.

"Fine. Al, will you come up here, please. Here's my chair, and here's a box with four bricks in it. I'd like you to hold the box and climb up on my chair and then down from my chair, and I'd like you to do it ten times."

Al looks at the class, grins, shrugs his shoulders and begins. About the fourth time, he begins making faces. He completes the task, puts down the box, and very dramatically falls to the floor in a stage faint. The class and the teacher laugh with him.

"Thank you, Al. Tell me, would you have done better without the bricks?"

"I'd have done better without the whole box!"

"Well, that was one of the problems that the rebel army was having. They were hot, because the temperature was in the high 80's during this time, and they were tired."

"I bet they were!" Al adds. Everyone laughs again.

"So, they began throwing things away that were heavy: Their cooking kits, tents, and their canteens when they were out of water. Some, as Al suggested, even threw away their whole back packs. Now, look at the map on page 138 of your books. What's on the other side of the mountains?"

"Farms!"

"And what's on a farm?"

There are several answers. Included among them are "food" and "water."

"Do you think General Lee's men need these things? And how will they get them if they do?"

"They'll come and take 'em."

"Right," says the teacher, "and to do that, they have to leave the mountains. By the way, Mary, what's the temperature in here?"

"78!"

"Why that's nothing! It was much hotter than that during the battles."

"How hot was it?" Jason asks.

"How hot? Jason, you'll find that in the encyclopedia under the Battle of Gettysburg. Why don't you look it up and tell the whole class. In the meantime, Barbara, will you pass out these stones, please."

Jason and Barbara go about their respective tasks.

"It was 87 degrees to 96 degrees on those days," Jason yells from the bookcase.

"Well, I guess 78 is enough for us," states the teacher, "shall we turn off the heater?"

The class roars its approval. By now Barbara has passed out the stones.

"Thank you, Barbara. Now will each of you take your stone and put it in your shoe."

The children comply with a few giggles thrown in.

The teacher continues, "General Lee decided that his men needed the supplies and that they would go into the farmlands to get them. There was only one problem. They'd been marching for a long, long time, and their shoes were all cracked and broken. When that happens you get stones in your shoes. They had to march over thirty miles. We don't have to go thirty miles to know what they felt like. Let's just walk once around our desks."

As the students comply, a chorus of "Oh's" and "Ow's", all good natured, rise from the class.

"Now you tell me, what else beside food and water did General Lee need for his men?"

"SHOES!" comes the chorus.

"That's right. Then one of General Lee's scouts came back and told him of a place nearby that made shoes, where he could get all he needed. It was in a quiet, sleepy little town . . . called Gettysburg . . . "

The lesson would continue through the actual Battle of Gettysburg. The articles of clothing would be used to further illustrate, for the children, the problems the soldiers faced in the hot weather. Since the lesson would probably lapse over into a second day, the logical homework would probably be the reading of the text pages on the battle. All in all, however, this lesson is conceptually oriented, involves all of the students' senses as well as their minds, and will, most definitely, be remembered. This was one of the most dynamic lessons we have ever seen taught, bar none. Yes, it took work and knowledge of materials, but what truly outstanding lesson doesn't? As an example of superior teaching, we feel it can't be beaten.

Chapter 9

Teaching Discovery Through Measured Performance

When we went to school we had a test every Friday. That meant that every Thursday night would find us "cracking the books" in preparation for the Friday ordeal and cramming our heads with material—most of which we had happily forgotten by Monday. Those things which we do recall and carry with us even today were those which we learned and used, those things which we needed to carry us forward toward a goal, not merely facts memorized to please our teacher and pass a test. As teachers, we should all concentrate on making learning a day-to-day activity.

HOW TO MAINTAIN CONSISTENT PERFORMANCE

Consistent performance in students is not an unattainable goal, despite what certain students may have proven to the contrary. For the vast majority of the students will maintain a consistent performance in our class provided certain guidelines are followed. We must make sure that the students do what they can use, that their work is directly related to what they are doing in class, that some assignments are student-generated, that students are required to think, that student material be used on tests, and that students are made to feel that what they have done before is helping them *now,* and that it may be applied in the future.

Students will do what they can use. If we give them tasks, notes, homework, etc. that are directly related to what they are using in class, then the work will come in. It is the assignment which seemingly has no meaning that is half done or not done at all. Consequently, we must make certain that students understand the relevance and need for an assignment. A homework assignment given only for the fact that the class will have an assignment is not only absurd, but it is counter-productive as well.

At least one out of every four assignments should be generated by the students themselves. If a student sees a particular need for something, he is already motivated to do it. If, for example, in the sample lesson given in the last chapter, a student had asked what exact route Lee had taken from Maryland to Gettysburg, asking a few students to prepare a map charting the route is a natural assignment, and one that *will be forthcoming*. There is no rule which states that all assignments have to be for the entire class. Gear some assignments to individuals based on their curiosity, and we have taken the first step toward winning the battle of productivity.

As far as questions that require students to think, we spent a great deal of the last chapter on just that. Make the students come up with reasons. Do not allow them to "buckshot" or guess. If they don't know, perhaps this is a point of natural motivation for an assignment.

Allow a certain amount of student work to be used on tests. Open notebook, homework assignments, projects, and other student-prepared materials which are incorporated into tests allow the students to discover that they can use what they have done.

Undoubtedly, you will tell them all of this in September. They will not believe you. Consequently, prepare your September materials around student work. Allow student mistakes to occur early in the year when they can learn and profit from them. Once they have learned the value of consistent work, they will produce it, and one of the major areas of student and teacher frustration and bickering will have vanished.

METHODS OF INCREASING
THE STUDENT'S UNDERSTANDING
OF THE IMPORTANCE OF HOMEWORK

We have talked about how the students can see the value of homework if they are allowed to participate in its selection and use. Now, the problem becomes one of how to handle this in a classroom situation and still continue with the scheduled material; we don't want to be on page 28 in June.

The following techniques have worked on multiple levels, grades, and ages. They solve the problem of allowing for student spontaneity and participation while continuing with the classroom material. The first one is called:

> IT'S YOUR CHOICE—The material to be covered is divided into, perhaps, ten assignments. The students are told to pick five or six from the ten presented. The assignments are geared to various skill levels and involve multiple activities. In selecting and doing *their* choice of homework, there is built-in motivation. Moreover, the assignments are coordinated with what is being taught by the teacher in class. The "master list" of assignments should be changed every week or so in order to keep the material fresh and ever-moving. The assignments may include such varied activities as skill work, graphs or charts, vocabulary and definition work, time or number lines, mini research projects, or drawing a picture or cartoon.

We pass along a word of advice about this technique from its contributor, Ms. Georgia Doyle. Make certain that the assignments are varied enough that everyone may take part. Ms. Doyle suggests that if you use ten assignments, three are so geared that *everyone* in the class may do them, another three are so constructed as to require more intensive thought and present a more difficult challenge, and the remaining four be aimed at the median ability of the class.

Another technique which has proven effective in accomplishing our purposes is called:

> IT'S YOUR TURN—A list of the topics to be covered in a unit is given to the class. A student selects one of the topics and is responsible for previewing it for the rest of the class. He can do this by showing or drawing a map, reading outside material, suggesting a film strip if available, he can write a story, etc. The student must do this according to certain guidelines set up by the teacher. It must be accurate (he must list his sources), and he must be able to defend his presentation after the class has learned the material. Previews must be given one or two days before the class gets to the actual material. In this way, students acquire responsibility, provide their own motivation, and they get a chance to see what it is like to teach. Picking the students at random will insure that the entire class is kept on its toes.

An added activity might be to have the students who have gone before evaluate the performance of the teaching student. Since they know how hard they had to work for their presentation, they can easily ascertain whether or not a student has properly prepared.

This final technique allows students a say in their own evaluation. It is called:

> IT'S YOUR TEST—The teacher announces that there is going to be a test on the material covered in the unit. The unique part, however, is that the teacher *and* the students will make up the test. Students are given paper and told to select the three most important facts or pieces of material that they have gleaned from doing their homework. If the homework that has been given is the natural outgrowth of work done in the classroom, there should be no problem with this. After sufficient time, the students turn in their papers one by one with no one else seeing the questions

except the student who has written them. After reviewing the student's papers, the teacher constructs the test. She may add those facts and concepts which she deems necessary for student understanding, but we suggest that no more than three additional questions be added. "Since everyone did their homework," the teacher comments, "everyone should pass this test." The passing grade will reinforce homework in the traditional method of approval (A's, B's, C's), while the making of the test will make the students feel a *real* part of the evaluation process and teach them the skill of extracting pertinent information from a complex whole.

The first time you attempt this technique your results will be less than perfect. The object is to have no student's questions left out of the test. Even allowing for duplications, that first test will be over long and contain extraneous material. By the third test, however, you will find that students are beginning to pinpoint and really are getting the most important factors from the unit. This technique not only involves students in the testing process, but offers three additional benefits: Homework will begin to be done completely and well; classroom participation will increase; and, the attentiveness to actual lessons will improve tremendously. When these goals are accomplished, there will be an additional side effect: Classroom management problems decline dramatically.

TECHNIQUES FOR GETTING STUDENTS
TO USE WHAT THEY HAVE LEARNED

Students should also be challenged to discover where their new knowledge can take them. If, for example, they have been studying how a hydra moves or how cilia is used for locomotion, pose them a question such as, "How does a person stay afloat while treading water?" Any practical extension of what is being taught will not only make the students think but will show them the value of their new knowledge.

Whenever possible, teachers should suggest further avenues of

exploration when a particular lesson has been completed. If a
lesson had a dog in it, for example, suggesting several authors
who wrote stories about dogs may provide the key for a great
deal of student enjoyment and enrichment. Also remember that
there is nothing wrong with *mentioning* material that may be
above the level of some students. Don't stress it, but if students
are encouraged to "reach," they just may "touch."

Also, any game that gives students a chance to correlate
material they have learned is of great advantage. Following are
two such activities which may easily be adapted to your grade
level and material:

I'M THINKING OF A PERSON (PLACE, THING, NUM-
BER)—Starting with the teacher, something is described in
parts. The student who determines what it is *and can add at
least two more facts about it,* gets to give the next one.
For example, the teacher says, "I'm thinking of a character
in a book. Here are three facts. He lived in Missouri; he
tricked some other boys in the neighborhood into helping
him paint a fence; and he ran away on a raft. Who am I
thinking of?" One child answers, "Tom Sawyer!" "Maybe," says the teacher, "give me two more things about
him." "He had an Aunt named Polly," says the student,
"and he smoked a corn-cob pipe." "Sorry, but one of
those things doesn't apply to him." "I know," another
student pipes up, "It was Huck Finn who smoked the pipe.
Tom had a girl friend named Becky, and he got lost in a
cave." "Right," the teacher answers, "He is Tom Sawyer.
Now you give us one." The game continues. Notice,
however, that the half-right answer couldn't be used again,
and the reason why it was wrong had to be given along
with two new facts.

CAN YOU GET THERE FROM HERE?—This game is
quite successful if students have been studying a particular
country or state or have been working on map skills. It can
also be done with anything which requires sequential
reasoning. Working together in groups or individually, the
teacher gives the students a point of departure and a

destination. Students then have to get to the destination in either the quickest time, shortest mileage, or with the least number of interruptions as the teacher may direct. The students call out as they arrive and their choice of route is explained to the rest of the class. Needless to say, they must be accurate. If the first answer isn't then the next group gets a chance, etc. Have four or five of these ready so that the process may be repeated and everyone may have a chance to participate. This not only works for geography and map skills, but has been successfully adapted in other subjects: "Who can get me from larva to butterfly?" "Who can get from meters to yards?" "Who can tell me how I got from Sherwood Forest to Nottingham Fair?"

The object of these or any games is not strictly the recall of fact but the reinforcement of the process of thinking something through to a conclusion and expressing it in the most succinct way possible. These are techniques which not only review the material but add form and direction to the thinking process as well.

Another way of getting students to use what they have learned is to make sure that the introduction of new material closely follows what the students have already learned. For example, if you are starting to study the Virginia Colony after studying the Massachusetts Colony, remember to use comparisons as a way of reinforcing previously covered material.

The next chapter will be on projects, and just to preview for a moment, it is this type of activity that best calls upon the student to use his knowledge to the fullest and to build with it and upon it.

INNOVATIVE TECHNIQUES
FOR NOTE TAKING

Note taking is a definite skill, and like other skills, it must be taught and it develops with use. That it is of value goes without saying, but there seems to be a prevalent misconception that it

is restricted only to the higher grades. We can think of no
reason why, after a child has learned to read and write, he
cannot be introduced to the beginning skills of note taking. It
should become an educational habit as easy and as acceptable as
signing one's name. It will if teachers take the time to teach
note taking as a skill and reinforce it in day-to-day classroom
situations.

Please understand, we are not suggesting that a second grader
can write an outline of Tolstoy's *War and Peace*. However, there
is no reason why he cannot take down the price of a particular
item in the supermarket each time he goes shopping with his
parents and then determine if the price has risen or fallen over a
month's time. Certainly, he can take down the words he may
have mispronounced on a reading lesson and check them off as
he learns to pronounce them correctly.

Let's take a look at skills involved in note taking as they may
be taught throughout the elementary school years:

GRADES 2-3

WHAT TO TAKE DOWN—In the beginning the teacher
will be the instigator of what the child takes down.
Gradually, as the skill develops, the child will begin to
determine for himself what should be noted. At this stage
particularly, what the teacher directs the student to take
down must be of almost immediate use to the child. The
child must be made to see the connection between taking
notes and its value and use in class.

HOW TO TAKE IT DOWN—At this particular level
students must not only be told what to take down, but
they must be shown precisely how to note it. Here, the
teacher's aim is to teach order. Through the use of
composition books, file folders, mimeographed sheets,
etc., children must begin to learn that spelling notes go in
one place, math in another, and history in still another,
etc. They must begin to see the fundamentals of structure
developing.

HOW TO USE "TRIGGERS" FOR REMEMBERING—
This very basic skill should be taught here and reinforced in every subsequent year. A "trigger" is any device

which will help a student remember something, from the proper pronunciation of a word to a theorum in science. A trigger is, of its very nature, individual and the teacher must aid and urge students to develop their own. Here are a few which we have seen used:

—These were used by a second grader to remember the functions of the plus and minus signs. "+" meant to add, so he remembered that by "adding" the hump on top. "-" meant to take away, so the "bubble" was dropping off the bottom.

—When Joey had trouble reading the word "BANANA" because all the "N's" and "A's" looked alike to him, he wrote it in this manner in his book and was able to remember it.

—Sheila used this drawing to remember that the letter combination "PH" had the sound of "F" as in tele*PH*one.

For older children these triggers can be funny sayings such as:

Tom Paine had a lot of COMMON SENSE.

Only the Apache Indians HORSED around.

George Washington climbed a MOUNT to see his friend VERNON; Tom Jefferson played his MONTI-CELLO;

and Andrew Jackson lived like a HERMIT in his old AGE,

Groan if you must over these "punny" sentences, but will you forget them? Neither will the students.

GRADES 4-6

First, during these grades you will continue to reinforce what has gone before. There will, however, be less and less teacher direction in what to put down and how to put it down.

LEARNING TO PICK OUT PERTINENT FACTS—This is the place where students begin to learn to pick out essentials. The only way students can become proficient in this is by doing it. Give them a great deal of practice in this and expect that there will be poor results at first, until they have learned. Keep reinforcing this skill through open notebook tests, using notebook material for homework assignments, and frequent references to past notes during class work.

BECOMING RESPONSIBLE FOR INDIVIDUAL NOTES—In the early grades the notebooks or files can be kept with the teacher. From now on they are the student's responsibility. If you have been reinforcing note taking in the ways we suggested, students will begin to realize the vital nature of their individual notes.

GRADES 6-8

Once students have learned to pick out pertinent facts, you can proceed to other note-taking skills. We are assigning this to the later grades, but if you have a third grade class that is capable, there is no reason why you can't try the following with them as well.

CONSTRUCTING WORD OR PHRASE OUTLINES— Once pertinent facts can be picked out by students within a given unit, they begin to form a collection of facts. Now the task becomes one of putting this collection into some kind of order so they will not have to go through an entire list in order to find a particular fact. At this point students can be shown the value of outlining. If they already have skills in selecting pertinent material, they should now be able to go to their notes and select the *most pertinent items of information.* These will become the major headings of their outlines. Periodically, students should be given the opportunity, supervised by the teacher, to put their notebooks into outline form. As with the pertinent-facts skills, students learn outlining by doing it. It doesn't always have to be written: a class can orally outline pages from a textbook or a homework assignment while the teacher places their answers on the board. At other times, outlining a story or a chapter may prove invaluable skill work.

Not that this work has to be dry or tedious. Far from it. One teacher we knew would regularly give his classes a mimeographed sheet containing thirty or forty of the most inane facts you ever saw, none of which were true. Some of the statements read, "Paul Revere's wife's name was 'Pickles,' " "Paul Revere liked to play pinball machines," and "Paul's grandfather played right tackle for Notre Dame." Then, the sheet contained statements like, "He was a member of the Son's of Liberty," "He warned the farmers of Middlesex that the British were coming," and "He got his signal from Old North Church." With all these "facts" in hand, students were required to place them into outline form under the general heading of "Paul Revere." Even though some statements were ludicrous and absurd, they began to find their way into the proper headings such as PAUL REVERE'S FAMILY (Remember his wife, Pickles?), REVERE'S SOCIAL LIFE (don't forget the pinball machines), and REVERE'S PLACE IN THE AMERICAN REVOLUTION. Not only was it great fun, but it reinforced and developed outlining skills. We hasten to add that this teacher had covered the material sufficiently that students were quick to realize which facts were real and which were not.

Let us say a few words about the type of notebook students can best use to take notes. If the material taken as notes is going to be interchangeable between subjects or units, then the ring binder is best. If the notes are going to be used on a continuing basis, a composition book of the marble cover type is excellent. It should be one book per subject or, in a Multi-Discipline Approach, one book per unit. Finally, when the whole notebook is a record and the most students will use of it is the material perhaps a month back, the Duo-Tang (soft cover) type seems best. A suggestion: Most teachers use the Duo-Tang books with the bendable prongs to the back. Why not keep the books with the prongs to the front where new material can be added *on top* of old material and is readily available. Adding sheets of colored paper between sections will further aid the student in selecting exactly what he needs when he needs it. The Duo-Tang cannot be used for interchangeable notes, and can only contain one subject's material.

Finally, a word of philosophy about student notebooks: With the exceptions of scientific pictures, map conceptualizations, graphs, or time lines, a notebook should *not* be used by any student other than the one who made it. Furthermore, no notebook should ever be picked up and evaluated by a teacher on any other basis than *can the child use it.* To assign a mark for a notebook on the basis of neatness, correct spelling or punctuation, doodles in the margin, etc., is to defeat the entire purpose of note taking. Do you want to evaluate a student's notebook? Give an open notebook test. If the child can pass using his notes, then his notes are adequate. If not, then a conference with the individual student to reinforce the skills that *he* needs will also suffice. At such a time it should be made clear to the student that he let his notebook down, not that his notes let him down. The care and feeding of a notebook is a student's responsibility!

BLUEPRINT FOR THE TOTAL STUDENT

In this and the preceding chapter, we have tried to give ways to increase the motivation and productivity of students. Let's see what kind of a student we've created.

Here is our *total* student:

*** He can take what he can use and apply it to something else, whether the material is actually related or just uses the same principles . . .

*** He can take his skills and build with them . . .

*** He can take pertinent material, conceptualize it, and make it his own . . .

***He can use the resources of a library, a dictionary, or an encyclopedia; of experimentation; or of the logical questioning of another, using the information he has to get to the bottom of what he wants to know . . .

*** He can compile and use his research to spur his recall and fit new data into the overall pattern of knowledge . . .

***He can take that pattern of knowledge and realistically probe for new knowledge . . .

Take this blueprint of the total student and add to it social awareness, responsiblity, self-discipline, and internalization of socially acceptable norms, and you have the ideal product of any school system. Of course, we all realize that this doesn't come overnight. We all do the best we can. We know we have to work at it from the moment the child enters kindergarten to the day he leaves our school forever. Yes, we all have problems; but no, they are not insurmountable. If we, as educators, all work together for a final goal, it will be achieved. Let it start with us.

"THIS IS MY FRIEND, PETER PENCIL"

Recently, we had an eight-year-old house-guest for an afternoon while her mother went shopping. She asked if she could watch television and indicated the program she wanted to see. We turned on the cartoon show as she continued, "It's an assignment from our teacher."

"Oh, really," we said, smiling at each other.

"Yeah, Peter and I have to watch this program."

Looking around the room and thinking we may have lost a child somewhere, we asked, "O.K., who's Peter?"

"This is Peter," she said holding up a pencil. "He's Peter Pencil, and he's gonna help me find out something."

She then proceded to take a pad from her bookbag, lie on the floor and begin to watch TV. Periodically, she would write on the pad. When the program was finished, she turned it off and, returning to the pad, began counting. Fascinated, we asked her what she was doing.

"Peter and I just found out how many commercials there were in a half hour cartoon show. We also found out there were two doll commercials, three for games, and four for toys for outside. I gotta take this in tomorrow. The class is gonna do this for a week with all different kinds of programs. It's called Medium."

"Media," we corrected with our mouths hanging open.

"That's right," she said, "do you know about it, too?"

This anecdote illustrates how even young children, given the proper motivation and skill reinforcement, can begin the process of note taking and conceptualizing. Not only was this child learning the rudiments of the study of media, she was taking steps toward the correlation of material and the proper notation of it. Indeed, Peter Pencil *will* be her friend for life.

Chapter 10

Capitalizing on Discovery
Through Individual and
Group Projects

The project has been the stand-by of the teacher probably since the first kid entered the first public school. Can anything new possibly be said about them? We think so, particularly when they are examined from a slightly different point of view. In this chapter we are not going to give you actual projects to do; every teacher we know has a multitude of ideas and sources from which to draw. Rather, we are going to examine the entire concept of the project as a dynamic teaching tool. Through this examination, perhaps we will be able to look at the projects we assign in a new light and begin to see facets to the jewel which we had never noticed before.

CHOOSING THE APPROPRIATE
PROJECT

It has been our experience that most elementary school teachers *love* projects. Walk into any classroom and you will probably see various student projects prominently displayed. Given a guided tour, you will be told what that chart represents, what the box in the corner does, and how hard Billy worked to make that ant farm. These projects may *or may not*, however, be examples of the fullest use of the project as a discovery technique. For, while the teacher may, indeed, love the project, the child may not have learned a thing by doing it. There is a way to make certain that it has been an enjoyable educational experience, however, and that is to make each project *appropriate*.

By "appropriate" we mean that a project should be suited to an individual child's:

1. AGE GROUP—Make certain that the project is suited to the child's age group, neither too babyish nor too mature and sophisticated.

2. SKILL DEVELOPMENT—To assign a project requiring skills which the child does not possess is not only frustrating; it is self-defeating.

3. SENSE OF RELEVANCE TO MATERIAL—Students should be able to see a reason for their projects within the context of their studies.

4. USE OF IT IN THE FUTURE—A project from which a child gets nothing more than a mark in a grade book is a waste of time.

How can we make certain that the projects we assign are appropriate, that the child benefits from them, and that he gets some fun out of it along the way? Perhaps the first step is to look at the types of projects and the criteria for evaluation inherent in each one:

THE RESEARCH PROJECT—This project develops the skills necessary to do research. It is inherently either right or wrong. By the conclusion of the project the child has either learned to do research properly, or he has not. Of course, it should be understood that along with the skills in research, the material researched should be relevant.

HYPOTHESIS AND EXPERIMENTATION PROJECT— Here, there is no right or wrong providing the methodology was logical. In other words, if the child went about the experiments properly, he has succeeded, regardless of whether or not it worked.

THE MECHANICAL PROJECT—This type of project is basically the same as the last. The major difference is that if it works, the student must show why it worked, and if it failed, the student must show why it failed. While most students can follow a set of directions for experiments, not all students are capable of in-depth examinations of causes.

THE WRITTEN/ORAL/VISUAL PRESENTATION PROJECT—This is the type of project where the presentation is more important even than the material. The student learns to write what he is thinking, express it orally, or visually demonstrate it to the class.

Every kind of project we can think of fits into one of those four categories. It is now necessary that the teacher determine the guidelines for introduction of projects. There are three sets:

TEACHER STRUCTURED—For a variety of reasons, most projects are begun with the teacher saying, "You will do ... " The subject of the project has already been pre-selected; students have little or no choice.

STUDENT STRUCTURED—The teacher announces the general topic or area for projects, and students must then come up with particular topics, treatment, and approach to the subject.

GROUP STRUCTURED—The teacher is presenting material. She has made it plain that projects may be done at any time. Various groups during the course of the unit come up with ideas to be tested through projects: "We want to see if ... "

The final step in choosing appropriate projects is to determine what the project will do for the student who undertakes it. We put this under six general areas:

STUDENT CONCEPTUALIZATION—Internalizing and using what he has learned ...

SKILL WORK—Reworking of facts or skills learned in class but from a different approach ...

STRUCTURED DISCOVERY—The student is given the opportunity to explore, follow up a hypothesis, etc. ...

THE ABILITY TO WORK INDIVIDUALLY OR IN GROUPS—Some children have to learn how to work with others; some how to work alone ...

SELF-DISCIPLINE IN A TIMED EXPERIENCE—The student learns to schedule his time or materials, plan ahead, etc . . .

REINFORCEMENT OF STUDENT CREATIVITY—The student gains respect for his own creativity, ingenuity or skills . . .

If we use the above guidelines to make certain that the project is appropriate to the child, that it is the proper type from which the child might most benefit, and that we have introduced it in the best possible manner, then we have begun the outline that will lead to our student's success with projects.

HOW TO DETERMINE INHERENT PROBLEMS IN A PARTICULAR PROJECT

Planning, both by students *and* the teacher, is the key for overcoming potential project problems. Always have the students submit at least a paragraph or partial outline about their project *before* granting approval for work to start. Getting into projects, even for a few days, and then having to give them up for *any* reason only reinforces failure, not confidence and success.

There is only one exception to this idea that we can think of—if the project's main reason for existence is for the students to develop their powers of scheduling time and determining the amount of work necessary for the project. Then if they have to give it up, *that's* the lesson they will learn—not that they can't do projects, but that they need to prepare more carefully.

Knowing where problems may arise is one of the first steps to overcoming them. Each project has its own inherent problems, but there are some problems which may be common to all projects. There may be problems with projects during their:

SELECTION—There may be problems with the time needed, the materials needed, and the ability of the particular student to do the project . . .

COLLECTION OF DATA—Where will the student get his information? What if he relies on someone and is let down? Moreover, too many students may be doing the

FIGURE 10-1

TEACHER'S PROJECT GUIDE

TYPE OF PROJECT: *Hypothesis/Experiment-Written/Oral/Visual*

DESCRIPTION OF PROJECT: *Reports, dioramas, charts, maps, etc. correlating study of Westward Movement.*

UNIT OF STUDY: *Social Studies*

AIMS OF PROJECT: *Research Skills - Ability to work in groups - Aid student conceptualization - Use of student creativity.*

PROJECT TARGET AREAS: *Route of Pony Express*
Building of Trans-Continental R.R.
Study of Mississippi River in terms of West
Cattlemen vs. Sheep Herders
Ranchers vs. Homesteaders

INHERENT PROBLEMS: *Overlapping use of materials -*
Careful selection by certain students -
School library to be closed 3 days -

HOW PROJECTS WILL BE USED: *Parts of Westward Movement taught through projects.*
Quiz on projects during last week.
Display projects during Parent Conference Week.

TIME TO BE EXPENDED (INTRODUCTION TO COMPLETION): *2½ weeks.*

same projects and material may not be readily available . . .

COMPILATION OF DATA—What if the student can't follow an outline, can't sift pertinent data, and can't or won't do all the work required . . ?

PRESENTATION OF DATA—It may be necessary to check the student's speech skills, writing skills, and manual skills in light of the presentation he must make . . .

EVALUATION OF PRESENTATION—By what criteria will the teacher judge the completed projects? Do the students understand the criteria? Have you sufficiently built in relevance and growth?

If you will look at Figure 10-1 you will see a TEACHER'S PROJECT GUIDE. This form should be copied in your notebook and made out by you prior to the assigning of any projects. The form is self-explanatory, and all that is needed is to fill it out according to your particular circumstances. The value of this form is that it causes you to look at *all* of the ramifications of your proposed projects. We would suggest that you make several copies of this form so you will have a fresh one handy for each new project you wish to assign.

Figure 10-2 is called the TEACHER'S PROJECT EVALUATION SHEET. As soon as the student turns in his outline, this sheet is stapled to it. As the student progresses with his project, you will be able to make notations concerning the student's progress with his project on this sheet. This sheet will show three things: It will show whether an individual student is getting what you want him to get from a project; whether you or the child have under or over estimated his abilities; and, used in conjunction with the Skill Chart and the Skill Chart Diagram (Chapter 6, Figures 6-3 and 6-4), it will show the areas that need to be stressed either individually, by groups, or class-wide.

You will be able to pick up several interesting facts from the use of this sheet. Figure 10-2A shows you a child who is running into trouble very quickly. To force this child to continue with the project which she will obviously fail, will only be frustrating to you and the child. It would be better to

FIGURE 10-2

TEACHER'S PROJECT EVALUATION SHEET

STUDENT: *Sheila Martinson*

PROJECT AREA: *Social Studies*

NAME OF PROJECT: *Indians of Western Plains*

Type of Problem	When Encountered	Where Encountered	How Handled
Selection	1st day	Couldn't narrow subject	Trial & error outlines — Teacher guided to finally choose one.
Selection	3rd day	couldn't select proper materials	Asked father and received help.
Collection	7th day	Hadn't heard from library about requested book	Told to work around it — She did, but is becoming frustrated.
Collection	9th day	Couldn't find example to use	Now doing very little on her own.

A.

STUDENT: *Andrea Scholenz*

PROJECT AREA: *Social Studies*

NAME OF PROJECT: *The Conestoga Wagon*

Type of Problem	When Encountered	Where Encountered	How Handled
Selection	1st day	Wanted to take a different angle than suggested in outline.	Was told to prepare a corrected outline — teacher guided.
Collection	4th day	Reported all material was in but wanted to know where she could find more.	Told where, not what, to find — Student doing beautifully!

B.

have her drop the project and work on those skills she needs for her *next* attempt at a project. Figure 10-2B shows you a child who is fully benefitting from the project and should be encouraged to do even more. We suggest that you have these sheets mimeographed in sufficient quantity that they may be kept handy.

YOUR GUIDE FOR SEPARATING CLASS, SUBJECT, AND INDIVIDUAL PROJECTS

There are three distinctly different kinds of projects that are used in a classroom. They are:

1. THE INDIVIDUAL PROJECT—In the individual project, one student works on one thing for no one's benefit but his own. For example, the student prepares a chart listing the names and dates of the Monarchs of England in their order of succession.
2. THE SUBJECT PROJECT—In the subject project we find one or more students working for understanding of a subject, but for no one's benefit but their own. For example, within a project on the Monarchs of England done by a group, one child studies the House of Tudor, another the House of York, etc.
3. THE CLASS PROJECT—In the class project, one or more students do one thing for the benefit of the whole class. Their piece will be needed to complete a whole picture. For example, Billy researches England at the time Henry VIII became King, Mary and Judy research the role of the Church during this era, Tommy researches England's relationship to Spain, etc. When finished, the projects reflect a total picture of the life, times and reign of Henry VIII.

Once having decided what type of project to introduce, the kind of project selected will dictate its use. Because of its very nature, the individual project can only be used by the individual who did it. *His* skills are reinforced. *His* self-discipline is exercised while doing the project. *His* discovery is individually oriented. Any use by the class of this kind of project will, of necessity, be contrived.

The subject project must be presented in a small group format. Again, it will be the children in the *group,* this time, who will have their skills and knowledge reinforced. The class will be onlookers, and, as before, the situation for presentation will have to be contrived.

The class project will demand use by the class. It is not extraneous, but a continuation of the lessons of the class. Each member has his own skills reinforced, and he reinforces everyone else's as well. His discovery leads to another's discovery, and at the same time, what he learns from the rest of the class is greater than what he has learned by himself.

Perhaps from reading the above descriptions you can tell that we are rather enthusiastic about the class project. If this is so, it is because we have seen its many benefits demonstrated in the classroom. Let us examine its ramifications in your classroom.

GETTING THE MOST
OUT OF A CLASS PROJECT

Having defined the class project, let's examine some of its implications:

1. STUDENTS GAIN RESPONSIBILITY—They have to do their work because it is needed by someone else.
2. STUDENTS LEARN SUBORDINATION OF THE INDIVIDUAL'S WILL TO GROUP GOALS—They can't do any old thing. It must conform to the class's needs.
3. STUDENTS LEARN THE COLLECTIVE SUCCESS OF TEAMWORK—They come to perceive that together they have created something bigger and better and finer than any one of them could have done on his own.

Moreover, students pick up certain skills in a class project. They are:

1. HOW TO LIMIT AND EXPLORE—The student learns how to narrow his area of concern, and then how to learn as much as possible about it.
2. HOW TO PRESENT AND EXPRESS PRECISELY—His material must be accurate, and he must be able to

explain it so that someone else may benefit from what he has learned.

There is no limit to the field of concentration for a class project. Anything studied by the class may be used. Furthermore, because it is not extraneous, the motivation is already there. A well-planned, relevant class project has extremely high motivation and is a dynamic tool for discovery.

Sometimes a class project will leave a lasting impression. So dramatic was the impact of one such project, that a student who was then a part of it is now teaching Social Studies:

"We were studying the Yucatan Peninsula. The teacher announced that we were going to do projects on what we had heard about in class. She listed several topics, and I volunteered to make scale models of Incan and Mayan temples, tell where they were found, and explain their use. Other children volunteered for other topics. We were allowed to work alone or with a friend. The time that they were due was stressed over and over again.

"The day came, and we brought our projects to school. As I entered the class, I noticed that the seats had been rearranged and in the rear of the classroom was an enormous table on which was a large outline of the Yucatan Peninsula. I was told to put my temples where they belonged. Because I had done the research I knew exactly where to put them. Another student had traced the route of Cortez and was laying it out when I arrived. Our textbook had said that Cortez had passed the temples, and as I placed my model, it intercepted the route! The other child and I were delighted. What we had read in the textbook had suddenly come true for us with new meaning and impact!"

A class project, creatively presented, can help students conceptualize many aspects of what they have studied in class. Their discovery is well worth your time.

USING CLASS TIME FOR PROJECTS—
A TEACHER'S GUIDE

The argument continues among teachers as to whether students should be allowed class time for projects. Some say that a project is a student activity and should be done on the student's time. Others argue that class time spent on projects allows for teacher aid and ready access to materials. We feel that by analyzing the kind (individual, subject, class) of project, a step toward solution may be taken.

An individual project is an individual's responsibility. Consequently, perhaps one class period to discuss problems, set students on the right track, suggest materials, etc., should be sufficient.

Because subject projects usually require group work, two or three periods may help to overcome some of the problems of the availability of group members to each other while allowing for teacher aid and direction.

The class project is different. The students are working as a class, even if they are working on individual parts. They are working on material relevant to their learning, and something that they will all use. Moreover, since the teacher is the only one who knows how the whole thing will fit together, she must be available both as a resource person and as a guide or leader to keep everyone on the right track. Consequently, class time for a class project is a must.

Class time is a precious commodity and should not be wasted. Some teachers feel that if they have not taught a lesson that day, they *are* wasting time. We are certain that this is *not* the case if a day is planned, relevant, and leads to a student's discovery.

HOW STUDENTS CAN USE
FINISHED PROJECTS

Once a student has finished a project the question should not be what can *you* do with it, but what can *he* do with it? We believe that if a student can't use it, or gains no physical satisfaction from it, or if it does not lead him to discover something new, then, in all frankness, the time devoted to the project was wasted.

Let's examine those three ramifications of the student use of the finished project:

    1. HE MUST BE ABLE TO USE IT—By "use it" we mean that through the project the student either:

      a. Gains something in his classwork . . .

      b. Reinforces a skill or skills he can use directly related to the project . . .

      c. Is helped to pass a test or recall some type of material . . .

      d. Reinforces a positive self-image . . .

2. HE SHOULD GAIN PHYSICAL SATISFACTION FROM IT—With the completed project the student should be able to:

      a. See it displayed . . .

      b. Be allowed to play with it either by himself or with others . . .

      c. Gain some satisfaction from the ability to say, "That's mine!"

3. HE SHOULD DISCOVER SOMETHING NEW—The completed project should spur the student to:

      a. Want to find out more about his or someone else's project . . .

      b. Gain new insights into similar situations related to his project area . . .

      c. Learn the correlation of material and become aware that one step leads to another . . .

Please understand, a child would not phrase it in this manner and does not go through these mental steps. We have never heard a child state, "My goodness, teacher, I have gained great satisfaction from this fascinating project!" However, if all the teacher does is pick up his project, put a grade on it, and hand it back, the child may feel disappointed without ever knowing why he feels that way. This vague disappointment may surface, however, in his lack of application to the next project.

Children need positive reinforcement in all aspects of their lives. Projects are no exception. Indeed, because of the time and effort involved, it *can't* be an exception.

Obviously, knowing what is needed by the child will suggest possible uses of projects to the teacher. For example, if the project were a diorama, a child would want to see it displayed as a three-dimensional representation of something that the class is studying. Perhaps he could show it to them so they could see "what it really looked like." Or, suppose a student did research in an area in which another student in the class is somewhat weak. Assigning the student who did the project to tutor the other student may prove of tremendous value to both of them.

Yes, projects are difficult to plan; yes, they are time consuming; but yes, they are a valuable tool in aiding the child's growth.

"I'M MAKING PEN-MY-SILLY-IN"

We have looked at all the implications of projects in the classroom. All, that is, but one. Projects may also have their lighter side. Over many years in the classroom we have heard many student comments, all delivered straight-faced of course, about projects. Allow us to share some of them with you:

"I'm making Pen-my-silly-in, and my sister is allergic to mold. What do I do?"

"I can't bring in my project on fleas, because my mother washed the dog!"

"If I feed the tadpoles a lot, will they turn into dinosaurs?"

"Oh, those stains! Well ... see ... my brother didn't know what it was, and the kitty litter box needed changing ... "

"I know it should be red, white, and blue, but the baby ate the red crayon!"

"Can you die from eating paste?"

"After I broke the ant farm and my mother dropped the casserole on my father's foot, they said I couldn't do that project any more."

"I couldn't reach the encyclopedia, so I made it up!"

"I know it looks like a blob of red paint on a piece of paper, but it's a graphic representation of social unrest in America!"

"I think I should get higher than a C+ after all those books I copied from!"

We are sure you'd have a few to add as well. They are fun, aren't they?

Chapter 11

Discovery Techniques
That Teach
the Underachiever

No matter how dynamic the lesson plan or how enthusiastically it is presented, every teacher has been faced with those students who, with the possible exception of the sound of their breathing, seem to be permanently mentally absent. These students, the underachievers, are a constant source of frustration to teachers. Nothing seems to get through to them. Assuming that every method short of physical force has been tried to help this student, and they have all failed, what else can the teacher do?

YOUR GUIDE FOR DEFINING
THE PROBLEM

Perhaps a clear definition of terms would be a good starting point. "Achiever" indicates a student who is assimilating knowledge and using it to gain more knowledge. Usually, this student participates well in class and is probably in the grade range from high "C" to low "A." Now, add the work "under," and you have a student who is *not* gathering necessary knowledge, *not* actively participating in class, and one who, with each passing day, lowers his grade potential. It is with this particular student that our problem lies.

Notice that nowhere in our definition did we state that the student *could not do* the work. A child with a learning problem

163

is one who, for various discernable reasons, *cannot* maintain a successful performance in the classroom. Many schools have hired Learning Disabilities Specialists to work with these children. There are innumerable techniques for aiding this type of student, and we have found that classroom teachers usually have unbounded patience and perseverance when dealing with the child who *can not do* the work. Our concern at this point, however, is the *underachiever* who needs specialized techniques to realize the *attainable* goal of becoming a productive student.

If we have a student in our classroom who we think displays the characteristics of an underachiever, our first step is to determine if the child has any disabilities which prevent his learning. Here, our Guidance facilities, Child Study Team, or Learning Disabilities Specialist can be of service to us. Also, checking with the school nurse may give us insights into any physical difficulties connected with the lack of performance. If, when all reports are in, there is a definable block to the child's learning either psychologically, emotionally, or physically, then the child should be reported to the proper agency within the school where he may receive the proper help. If, however, all reports are negative, we probably have an underachiever on our hands.

CHECKLIST FOR UNDERACHIEVEMENT

Let's look at some of the symptoms which the underachiever exhibits. They are:
  *** Poor, inconsistent, or incomplete homework . . .
  *** Inability to answer oral questions given during classroom review . . .
  *** Poor test scores on material previously covered in class . . .
  *** Inattentiveness in class . . .
  *** Major or minor classroom disruptions . . .
  *** Character violations such as lying, cheating, etc . . .
  *** Poor mental attitudes either toward or from his classmates.

Not all underachievers display all the symptoms listed, and you may have a few more to add, but exactly pinpointing the symptoms of *your* underachiever will give you the clues as to which of several discovery techniques might do the most precise good for him in light of his particular needs and problems.

Let's take two examples:

Larry is an underachiever who is a constant source of minor classroom disruption. He is also very erratic in turning in homework assignments. That which he completes, however, is done correctly if not neatly. You further note that on those days he has done almost all of his homework, he causes practically no problems in the classroom. Apparently the point at which to begin expanding Larry's potential would be in getting him to do more consistent homework

* * *

But look at Jane. She almost never does homework, and even when she turns it in, it is obvious that *she* did not do it. When confronted with a test, Jane either puts her name on the top of the paper and nothing else, blatantly tries to cheat, or guesses at a rate that strains the laws of chance. This same uncaring attitude has also gotten her into difficulties with several of her classmates through tattling and lying. The point at which to begin helping Jane would appear to be with her own self-concepts.

Even though Larry and Jane are both underachievers, the techniques needed to help each are different. Each underachiever is an individual and, as such, is unique and has unique problems. Techniques to aid the underachiever, therefore, must be geared to handle what is needed for a particualr individual. This understanding of different requirements is the cornerstone for pinpointing the most beneficial technique. All underachievers are not alike, and to use blanket techniques to handle them gives the classroom teacher less than an even chance at success. Consequently, the first step is to pinpoint the particular problems experienced by *your* underachiever.

A UNIQUE DEVICE FOR PINPOINTING
UNDERACHIEVERS' PROBLEMS

Because a classroom teacher's time is so valuable, we must take care that when describing a method for pinpointing underachievers' difficulties, the method be practical, efficient, and worthwhile. It was to this end that several years ago we devised the graph shown in Figure 11-1. Before we get into how it works, allow us to explain why it was developed.

Just as there is an old maxim which states, "The journey to Mecca begins with the first step," so it has been our experience that a basic pattern of success always begins with a first major success. We have seen this illustrated in so many cases with so many children over the years that we have come to accept this as fact.

Our belief in this statement demands that a child's problem be separated into distinguishable parts in order that we could determine which part he could most easily conquer, for it followed that if the child succeeded once, was given positive reinforcement, and encouraged on to the next task, each part of the problem would eventually lead to the total solution of the student's difficulties.

No piano teacher, for example, would begin a student with a study of the theory of advanced harmonics. First the child learns a song. Even if it is as simple as "Mary Had A Little Lamb," the child has succeeded and upon that success his future study of music will be built. So, too, a child who has constantly met with academic failure has established a pattern of failure. If, however, he can succeed in something, no matter what, then that success can be made to provide the impetous for breaking the pattern of failure, and we can begin to build his future successes. Obviously, then the first step had to be some method of clearly exposing the problems and also *their order of importance and solvability*. The result was the graph which you see pictured in Figure 11-1.

Let's look at that Figure. Across the top you will see listed the possible component parts of a *totally* underachieving student. Down the left-hand margin, you will see gradations from one to ten, with one indicating the best and ten showing the worst.

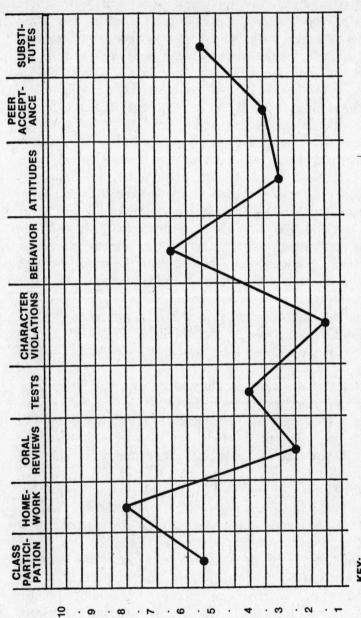

KEY:
Always Poor — 9, 10; Almost Always Poor — 7, 8; Generally Not Up To Par — 4, 5, 6; Almost Always Good — 2, 3; Never A Problem — 1.

FIGURE 11-1

Now take a look at *your* underachiever. Using the key material at the bottom of the graph, assign a mark for where you believe his performance fits under each of the given categories. We suggest that if he is always poor in a category, you assign a nine or ten; almost always poor—a seven or eight; generally not up to par—a four, five, or six; almost always good—a two or three; and never a problem—a one.

The key point here is to be objective. If Alex totally disrupted the class on the day you decide to start the chart, but he is not a usual classroom disruptor, be certain to view his *total* performance and not the one day incident. Granted, it is extremely difficult to be objective about someone who has just poured ink over your prize geraniums, smeared chewing gum in Betty Lou's hair, and written "Teacher Is A Rat Fink!" on the blackboard, and if all that has happened, perhaps it would be better if you waited until the next day! In any case, take your student and completely work him through the graph. We have found that the actual time spent in doing this is less than five minutes.

When you have finished, join the marks by straight lines. Your graph should now look something like Figure 11-1, which is one we ran on Larry, the example we used earlier in this chapter.

The value of the graph should now be apparent. At a glance you can determine which problem to attack first. Remember, the idea is to occasion a first success and then build upon it. Take the most blatant, obvious, and *easiest-to-solve* problem first, for if you take the most difficult there is a possibility of failure.

In Larry's case (Figure 11-1) it is obvious that he has very little problem with character violations, and although there are some difficulties with oral reviews, tests, attitudes and peer acceptance, they do not appear to be severe enough to be significant. His major problems lie with substitute teachers, general behavior, class participation, and particularly home-work. Add this to what you have gleaned from observation (in this case, from the example we used earlier), and homework does become the logical place to start.

Whatever the graph may look like for your particular under-achiever, remember that what you are looking for is the discovery of success, and *that* will engender more success. Indeed, we found that it was entirely possible that by success-fully overcoming minor problems, the child *discovered* his own solution to a major one.

HOW TO IMPLEMENT DISCOVERY TECHNIQUES FOR UNDERACHIEVERS

Throughout this book we have tried to give adaptable discovery techniques, be they from subject to subject, grade to grade, or classroom to classroom. The following are three examples of techniques we found useful with the underachiever. As you read them, consider how they might apply to you and your underachiever in your particular set of circumstances. You may have found one earlier in this book or have one of your own which you could adapt, but here are ours:

MR. SMART—This is a technique used to get more, properly done homework. Dan never turned in homework, and when he did, you couldn't read it. We found that he really did understand most of the material, but just didn't do the work. On the first day we let Dan read a simply worded explanation of what "IQ" meant. Then we took what there was of his homework for that day and told Dan that we were going to use it as an "IQ Test" and grade it on a scale of 0 to 150. Dan's paper rated about Moronic on the IQ scale.

"Gosh," we said, "That doesn't look so good. Do you think you're like that?"

"No!" he answered. "That ain't fair; you gotta give me another chance!"

"Well . . . " we said, inwardly rejoicing at his enthu-siasm.

"Com'on, ya gotta!"

"O.K., we'll try again tomorrow."

Dan's homework the next day showed he had taken

more time, but it was still below normal. Something like
the previous dialogue ensued again, and we kept at it.
Subsequent periodic checks showed that Dan had progressed to the point where he was fast approaching
"genius" rating in his well-done, neatly-completed homework.

IF I HAD A FRIEND—This technique was used to aid the
child with underlying personality difficulties that were
hampering his academic success.

"Jack," we said, "we want you to complete this statement, 'If I had a friend, he would be . . . ' "

It took some prodding, but Jack began to list qualities
like honest, funny, wouldn't squeal, would stick by me,
etc. We dutifully recorded each response, and pushed until
he had given us everything he thought a friend should be.
We then took his responses and turned them into questions
related to and directed at him, such as, "When somebody
got in trouble today, did you try to help instead of just
laughing at them?"

Almost all his responses were negative, but about half
way through the list his eyes grew wide. It was an amazing
thing to witness. It was almost as if we could see into his
mind as the realization came over him that what he most
admired he was most unlike. Finally, we gave Jack the list
of his own responses and kept a copy for ourselves. We set
him the task of becoming the person he had described. We
gave him our word that we, too, would follow his list and
help him as he helped himself.

THE SIDE-BOARD TACTIC—Whenever we set the table
from the side-board, we would put out the plates only to
find we had to return to the side-board to get the
silverwear, only to return to get the napkins. In other
words, one task engendered another. When Tommy told us
that all he wanted to do was fix cars, we got him a
complicated model of a car. We helped him of course, but
we didn't do it for him. We would put glue on a particular
part or hold something until it dried, but Tommy had to

tell us what went where. If he asked us, we would indicate the directions. Naturally, he had to improve his reading in order to understand those directions. Nor was the completion of the model the end of Tommy's learning experience. He had to go to his math book when we asked him how far that model would go on a gallon of gasoline, and he had to study geography when asked if he could get to Chicago or Los Angeles from Gary, Indiana on that same tank of gas. One activity, based on the child's curiosity and carefully guided by the teacher, can prove the springboard to helping the underachiever in a variety of subjects.

These are some of the techniques we used. Let us re-emphasize that whatever is used, it must be practical. No technique, no matter how good it looks on paper is worthwhile if it does not work for you or a particular child. If the physical necessities are unrealistic for your school's circumstances, if you cannot adapt it to your particular personality or the rapport you have established with an individual child, then select a technique that *will* work for you.

Also, a technique which goes on seemingly forever, has the negative effect of boring and fatiguing the student *and* the teacher. Make certain, therefore, that your techniques are not overly time consuming. For example, the technique called IF I HAD A FRIEND took fifteen minutes after school one day and about five minutes a week thereafter, and we only wish you could have seen the positive change in that student!

HOW TO CAPITALIZE
ON DAY-TO-DAY PERFORMANCE

We have already shown the need of success for the underachiever, but be advised that the success must be *real*, not manufactured or a "gift." To say that red is blue or that two plus two equal five is simply not true and everyone knows it. Likewise, to tell a child that he is doing well when he has gotten nine out of ten questions wrong is a lie—the teacher knows it, the class knows it, and, most importantly, the child knows it, too.

The idea is to find a point at which the child *really* does succeed and then to capitalize upon that *real* success. Nowhere can this be better done than in the day-to-day operation of the classroom.

Immediacy of positive reinforcement has always been a beneficial technique for accomplishing this goal. Let us say that Julie does not do homework often, but on this particular day you have noticed that not only did she do the assignment, but she did it accurately. *This* is the day to bring her to the blackboard. Now, rather than the ridicule or mild chastisement she receives for failing the assignment, she has been given positive, constructive signs of approval.

Suppose that Jeff usually daydreams his way through class, but today, for whatever reason, he has applied himself to the lesson being taught. This might be an ideal time to give a short quiz on the material covered that day. Because Jeff has studied and worked he stands an excellent chance of doing well. The quiz certainly won't hurt the rest of the class, and for Jeff it could be the starting point for the something even more important than his good mark in the teacher's grade book.

If we make certain that whenever a student conforms to our expectations, we deliver this constructive approval, we will be building in a pattern of success. Even if the student should occasionally slip, we will have shown our class that they can succeed. This discovery is as important to their educational growth as the retaining of the skills in a particular subject area.

Moreover, we will discover that *our* attitudes will change as well. All too often, because of daily pressures, the hectic nature of our profession, record-keeping and clerical necessities requested by administration, etc., we tend to acquire a negative outlook. We keep looking for what is wrong in order to correct it. Now, however, we will be looking for success, even small successes, and in this quest we will become intimately involved with our students. We'll collect assignments, not to see who didn't do it, but to see how well Jamie did last night. We are all well aware of how teacher attitudes carry over to the class. Build an attitude of success, and you can't help but succeed.

"THE CASE OF THE OPEN DOOR"

By this point in the book, you have undoubtedly gathered that we know many teachers. This is quite natural since our lives are involved with education. If there is one single feeling that we have gained from that association it is that while problems will always be with us, so will their solutions. Sometimes these solutions are not at once evident, but given time, dedication, and the creativity of the individual teacher, they will be forthcoming.

As a case in point, we offer this true story which comes to us from a very dear friend:

" 'And where were you? Class started five minutes ago! '

" 'I know cloud formations are fascinating, but would you mind paying attention to what we're doing in class—just once!'

" 'If that paper airplane flies, so do you!'

" 'It's been fifteen days and fifteen different excuses. Doesn't *anybody* have their homework?'

"It was shaping up to be a miserable year. In the heat of September I had to keep my door closed so the noise wouldn't disturb the neighboring classes. Beautiful lesson plans never saw the light of day as I spent most of my time pulling kids off the ceiling! They were accomplishing nothing, and I didn't feel I was either. It was a complete disaster!

"Then I thought, 'I'm not a baby sitter; I'm a teacher, and a good one!' I decided to do something about it. Over one weekend, I sat down and analyzed the members of my class. I poured over every facet of my class, its good points and its bad. Monday morning I came in and changed seats. My desk went on another wall, and I announced that it was the beginning of September all over again. Armed with some discovery techniques, I began working with each member of my class on an individual basis. I stopped caring what my *class* did, and I began concentrating on Mary and Mark and Ronnie and Paula. By Friday, I had the small beginnings of a cohesive group. We were working together.

"I wish I could say it was all easy—it wasn't, and I'm still at it. However, the successes are coming faster now, and by the way, my door stays open most of the time."

We include this anecdote to show what can be done using positive, practical discovery techniques, especially when used by a dedicated, creative teacher. You may not have a *whole class* of underachievers; you may just have three or four. If that is the case, then start today to work with them as individuals, to see them as individuals, with the firm conviction that you *can* help. Believe us, their discovery of success will convince you that it is well worth the effort.

Chapter 12

Discovery
and the Exceptional Child —
A Teacher's Guide

"I have a student I want you to meet," Sue Mamchak said to her husband one night. "I think you'll be amazed."

"After the years I've spent in a classroom," Steve Mamchak answered, "I doubt it."

"O.K., wise guy, I'll bet you dinner out on it."

"You're on!" he said.

"IT'S A DISTINCT PLEASURE
TO MAKE YOUR ACQUAINTANCE . . . "

The next day was Friday and that afternoon Sue was holding a meeting of the school newspaper staff. Steve arrived about ten minutes into the meeting.

"And where is this exceptional child who is going to amaze me?" he asked.

"Right this way."

They walked across the room to a place where several children were busy assembling sheets of mimeographed paper.

"Allison, would you come here a moment, please."

One of the children broke fom the group. She was a diminutive child, perhaps nine years old, her freckled face beaming, her sparkling eyes a perfect match to her curly brown hair.

"Allison, this is my husband."

Steve bent forward and smiled. He was completely taken by

175

this charming child before him. "Hello, Allison," he said, "it's nice to meet you."

"Well," Allison replied, "so you're Mr. Mamchak. It's a distinct pleasure to make your acquaintance, Sir. Mrs. Mamchak has told me a great deal about you, and I've looked forward to our meeting. I trust you're in good health."

"Err . . . quite well . . . thank you . . . . err . . Well, Allison . . . err . . do you like being on the newspaper?"

"Indeed I do. In fact, I'd been considering journalism as a career, and this seems the ideal opportunity to see if . . . "

She continued on, but Steve wasn't really listening. With his mouth hanging slightly open he turned to his wife.

"O.K., Sue," he said, "where do you want to go for dinner?"

* * * * *

We start with this recollection as near to what actually happened as we remember it, for admittedly it was many years ago, because it exemplifies what happens the first time a teacher, even an experienced one, comes in contact with a truly exceptional, gifted child.

What a joy it would be to have such a child in your classroom. How wonderful, how marvelous, how easy, right? Not at all! The exceptional or gifted child may prove as great a source of frustration both to himself and the teacher as any underachiever or classroom disruptor. The gifted child has his own particular set of problems which demand specialized techniques for their successful   solution.

The pressures placed upon the exceptional or gifted child by his home, the school, his peers, and the very curriculum he must follow, are all sources of problems which must have pinpoint solutions if the child is to realize his full potential, not only in the academic areas, but in personality and social development as well.

EXAMINING OPTIONS FOR THE GIFTED CHILD

There seem to be two prevalent theories concerning the gifted child in the classroom. One theory sees him as cream to be separated and whipped into butter, while the other theory sees him as cream to be homogenized to make the milk all the richer. Whether the child should be separated and given a special environment or remain in the room with the rest of the class should not be predetermined. Each gifted child is an individual and should be treated individually. Some gifted children *do need* a specialized environment, while to isolate others would only prove detrimental. Consequently, each case must be judged on its own merits.

A second point of contention is the so-called "Room Theory." It goes something like this: "With one of those kids, you could take them, lock them in the library, come back four years later, and they'd have learned more than you could ever teach them!" This mistaken opinion, too often held even among educators, has set the education of the exceptional child back a hundred years. Holding to this philosophy, there is no need for an expanded curriculum, there is no need for additional funding for specially guided programs, and there is no need for special materials that will be used by only a few. Fortunately, recent changes are beginning to acknowledge that the gifted child has as many if not more needs than any other child, and particularly needs guidance, motivation, and structured situations in which to develop.

All too often the exceptional child finds himself frustrated by school-sponsored conformity: He has just discovered the ramifications of bacterial growth; everything within him cries out to push onward and discover more; his mind is filled with a thousand unanswered questions then the bell rings and he must be in his next class in three minutes. How frustrating!

Yes, the gifted child needs special handling, but not all gifted children are alike, nor do they have the same needs. Consequently, in this chapter we will attempt to pinpoint the six major types of exceptional children, examine the types of problems inherent in each, and through anecdotal examples try to propose some techniques for solution. We will also look at two methods which have been proven effective in dealing with gifted children, and finally, we will examine evaluative methods best suited to the particular child.

CHECKLIST OF EXPANDING TECHNIQUES
FOR THE "NATURAL DISCOVERER"

The first step in dealing effectively with the "natural discoverer" is for the teacher to discover what kind of gifted child this is. Let's look at what we conceive to be the six major types of exceptional children:

> THE UNI-SUBJECT EXCEPTIONAL—This is the child who does exceptionally well in *one* particular subject because of high motivation coupled with medium to high medium ability. He learns in a particular subject because he wants to. He will do math problems for hours, for example, but could not care less about English or Social Studies. His particular subject interest may or may not be easy for him.

Jerry enjoyed the mental gymnastics of math. Each time he learned a new skill, he would examine it to its limits. Consequently, through practice, he got to be better at math than anyone else in his class. His straight A's made everyone assume that he should be getting A's in his other subjects as well. This was not the case, however, since it was only his *motivation* and not increased ability that occasioned his high marks. What Jerry needed was increased motivation in his other subjects.

> THE UNI-SUBJECT GIFTED—This child seems to learn intuitively in one subject area. There seems to be no extraordinary motivation, intellectual background, or increased skills, yet the child learns at a phenomenal rate. He just seems to "know" it, because "it has to be that way."

Throughout her school career, Roxanne had been receiving C's with an occasional B here and there. Then she entered eighth grade science. As part of the curriculum there was the study of astronomy. When the class was told that Jupiter had twelve moons, Roxanne piped up, "Yeah, and they have to be all different sizes, don't they?" "Why would you say that?" her teacher asked. "Well, it just has to be that way. Nothing that big

could have twelve moons orbiting that were all the same size."
"How do you know that?" her teacher asked. "Did you read it
some place?" "No," came the answer, "but look at it. It just has
to be that way."

Roxanne proceeded to amaze everyone with her seemingly
intuitive knowledge and grasp of astronomy. Even complicated
theories seemed to her logical. Roxanne was allowed to pursue
her natural bent toward astronomy and it was discovered that
she soon filled in what she was lacking. Her language arts and
math skills skyrocketed, for example, because she needed them
for her research.

> THE PRESSURE-ORIENTED EXCEPTIONAL—This child
> does well in *all* his subjects but only through tremen-
> dous effort. He is the straight A student whom everyone
> conceives of as brilliant and able to do anything that is
> asked of him. His marks, however, come to him through
> hours of pressure-oriented work. Things do not come
> easy to this child, but he works at them like a man
> driven by demons.

Karen had everything; she was an "A" student, a cheerleader,
president of her class, feature editor of the newspaper, and
everyone's ideal of the perfect student. She also had an ulcer
and was making fast progress toward a nervous breakdown at
age twelve. Karen had to *work* to get her marks and do well in
her school activities. In a pressure-cooker environment, she
drove herself unmercifully because everyone expected her to do
well, and she couldn't let them down.

Barring the impracticality of giving this student a year off to
spend at the beach, her teachers, recognizing the danger signals,
began to minimize the pressures she was facing. Gradually, they
weaned her away from high pressure activities, Instead, they
made her a classroom tutor and allowed her to help establish a
classroom library. She was still given responsibility, but was
placed in those situations where it was not essential that she
"do or die."

> THE TRANS-SUBJECT GIFTED—This child seems to do
> well intuitively in all his subjects. There is no pressure

here, nor an inordinate amount of effort on the part of the student. They just do well. There is very little you can ask of them that they cannot do.

If you gave Neil an assignment he would bring it back to you five minutes later completely and correctly done and ask, "Now what would you like me to do?" Neil was the true gifted child. Anything his brilliant mind could conceive of, he could most likely do. He was at once totally frustrated and frustrating in a classroom. Fortunately, his school had developed an independant study program (described later in this chapter) which enabled him to progress at his own, accelerated pace.

THE MANUALLY GIFTED—This child can do anything with his hands. This is the child who may not be able to use the microscope, but he can take it apart and put it back together and tell you how it works. There is nothing, given the materials, he can't fix or build. His sense of spatial relationships, design, and the way things fit together to work makes him unique.

Danny didn't do his English assignment because he was busy working on his airplane. That is, the airplane he had conceived of, planned, designed, and was building. While he had not done his homework assignment on verbs, he had, on his own, read extensively about aviation, had written to the U.S. Air Force for information on design testing, and was keeping a voluminous notebook. Like Roxanne, Danny was picking up what he needed. The technique that worked for Danny was to let him explore the world of mechanics and discover his need for other subjects. When he discovered the need for something, he would acquire it.

THE "OUTCAST" GIFTED OR EXCEPTIONAL—This child is out of step with his surroundings. This is the child who, while he may be gifted or exceptional in one or all ways, does not get along with his peers, teachers, parents, or himself. He is the basically unhappy misfit. He is intolerant and intolerable.

Kevin liked no one, and no one liked Kevin. He was picked on and bedeviled by his peers. In turn, he could exact revenges that made Machiavelli look like Peter Rabbit. In a classroom he manifested a politeness bordering on insolence, and the lesson continued or not according to his whims. One more thing about Kevin—he was absolutely brilliant.

This child's need is not academic, but social. Before he can utilize the full potential of his mind, he must learn to control himself like any other classroom disruptor. The techniques must be carefully chosen, however, for this child is fully aware of what is happening to him. We solved one such problem by playing to a particular child's weakness. She was quite short, and we constantly assigned her tasks that required that she reach high objects. There were many taller children in the class, and she soon learned that politeness got her further than invective.

We hope you have noticed that throughout this section we have not used the terms "exceptional" and "gifted" inter-changeably. They are not the same. "Gifted" denotes innate ability. "Exceptional" denotes high motivation and/or ability. From here on, we will include both types of children under the term "natural discoverer." For the remainder of this section we will speak about the natural discoverer outside the classroom, and in the next section we will examine his role within the classroom.

Let's look at three techniques that have worked well with the natural discoverer when he is taken out of the classroom:

THE EXCEPTIONAL LEARNING CENTER—This is a place, be it a room, part of the library, converted store-room, etc., where a variety of materials for the natural discoverer have been placed. Here are the extra micro-scope, the Beethoven records, the works of Shakespeare, etc. that have been gleaned from any number of sources. If money is a problem in your school (and show us a school where it isn't!), this option has several advantages. The materials are given permanent housing, but they need not be acquired all at once. Discarded textbooks, contributions from teachers, parents, PTA groups, etc., secondary school throw aways, may all be sources of materials. Moreover, although designed for the natural discoverer, this center may be used by anyone else with a definite purpose. Nor does this center require special or additional personnel to staff it. It is a place where the natural discoverer may come and exercise his mind.

THE INDEPENDENT STUDY PROGRAM—The purpose of an independent study program is to provide the individual with an opportunity to program his own education in order that a "continual search for questions, awareness, measurement, and reality becomes a lifestyle."[1] Within such a program, the child works independently upon teacher-guided projects of his choosing. After selecting a particular field of study, the child writes up a contract detailing his initial goals and procedures which is reviewed and discussed before the final signing. He then proceeds to work on his project with regular meetings to discuss problems and progress.

Through such a study the natural discoverer learns to choose appropriate projects, choose goals and methods for his study, locate information from a variety of sources, take responsibility for his learning, organize his time and information, analyze and criticize, contribute new knowledge to his fellow students and teachers, and evaluate his product upon completion.

Within this type of program the student has the opportunity to make many choices, some of which will be poor. For the natural discoverer, however, this only serves to demonstrate the need for additional educational experiences and sends him forth with even higher motivation than before.

When an independent study program is fully working for the natural discoverer, it is a joy to behold.

We hope you understand that this highly condensed description of the independent study program cannot do full justice to its marvelous potential. Our thanks to Mr. John Pfeffer of Beck Middle School and Terry Janeczek of

---

[1]Beck Middle School Independent Study Program, 1972-1975, Cherry Hill, New Jersey

River Street School for opening our eyes to this very viable option of the natural discoverer.

SEMINAR FOR NATURAL DISCOVERERS—Students are given a syllabus containing an outline of what is being taught in the classroom. It lists all the requirements for a block of work from one to three weeks long. A seminar is held to discuss any potential difficulties with the work. Students now begin to work on their own. They must complete the work on the syllabus, but they are free to explore any ramifications of the material which they might discover. The teacher acts as a resource person.

At the conclusion of the block of work the student may take either a written or oral exam on this material, *including* the work he has done on his own.

This is a more structured approach than the independent study plan.

For these three options there are only two items that need concern us: availability of materials, and our school's policy on student time. As far as materials are concerned, we discussed that earlier. As for time policies, these must be worked out in your school. Those responsible for policy should understand that a natural discoverer learns all the time. His mind cannot and will not be forced to function only between one bell and another.

These options have worked well for the natural discoverer who has been removed from the classroom environment. If, however, you believe that this child is a greater benefit to himself and his peers if he remains in the classroom, you will find that you have several other options.

HOW TO USE THE NATURAL DISCOVERER IN THE CLASSROOM

Within the classroom the natural discoverer may be used to the advantage of himself and others in a number of ways:

RESOURCE PERSON/TUTOR—Particularly in heterogeneous groupings, the natural discoverer can help the discovery of others and reinforce his own through passing on what he has learned.

SUPPLEMENTARY "TEACHER"—The teacher may ask the natural discoverer to explain or elaborate upon a particular aspect of the material being covered by the class.

PARALLEL DISCOVERY—The teacher generates a project for the natural discoverer paralleling what is going on in class. The class learns from the outcome of this parallel project.

THE OPEN-ENDED ASSIGNMENT—This assignment is generated by the class. Someone asks how a light bulb works, for example, and if that same class contains a natural discoverer whose bent is science, you might have him explain it to the whole class. The question does not have to parallel what is going on in the class at that time.

REINTERPRETING MATERIALS FOR VARIOUS STIM-ULI—An area covered in class by use of the textbook, is then reinterpreted by the natural discoverer and presented to the class in another form of stimulation (diorama, short play, recorded cassette, etc.). This not only helps the preparer, it aids those children who may need more than one form of stimulation in order to learn something.

We have a very strong word of caution when using any one of these five techniques. *At no time should the natural discoverer prevent or interrupt the discovery process of any other member of the class.* There is nothing to prevent several children from looking up the same thing. The use of the team approach, particularly in parallel and open-ended assignments will effectively integrate more than one student into the discovery process. Students should not become lazy or apathetic just because there is a natural discoverer in the class. Rather, the natural discoverer should inspire even more discovery on the part of his peers. The class should stimulate and be stimulated by the natural discoverer.

MORE DISCOVERY—
NOT MORE WORK

Nowhere in this chapter or in this book are we using the word "discovery" to equate with "extra credit." The natural discoverer does not need extra credit assignments, nor does he need more work, nor does he need work given merely to keep him busy. What he does need are new avenues to explore, and new approaches over which to ponder. The natural discoverer will make his own work, and he will fast learn if that work is profitable. If we continuously give the natural discoverer work to keep him occupied until the class catches up, we will soon find that he will do no work at all.

Whatever techniques we use with our natural discoverer, make certain that they are aimed at:

1. ENLARGING HIS WORLD
2. EXPLORING AND EXERCISING HIS MIND
3. BRINGING HIM NEW AND MEANINGFUL CHAL-LENGES
4. PINPOINTING HIS FIELDS OF INTEREST
5. ALLOWING HIM TO BE CREATIVE

If we keep all of these goals in mind when assigning work for our natural discoverer, we will find that we will be starting him on the pathway to the recognition of his full potential.

DETERMINING THE BEST METHODS FOR
EVALUATING THE NATURAL DISCOVERER

In the vast majority of elementary schools today, three predominant forms of evaluation are used. The first is the standard report card. This form, using either a letter or numeric grade, shows the result of the child's work over a period of time as reflected in the criteria established by the school and the teacher. They are comparative (Johnny got an A; Mary got a C+). They do not show, aside from the rise and fall of a grade, what is happening to the student. The second form is the checklist. This is usually a list of skills and abilities which the teacher checks off as *the class* accomplishes them. This is even more arbitrary than the first form. The child may have already learned a skill but may not have it checked off until the entire class has covered it. The final form is the personal narrative, and it is usually incorporated with parent conferences. They usually combine a gradation (Excellent to Poor, for example) with a personal explanation of the mark. The effectiveness or weakness of this system is entirely dependent upon the participants.

While any of these evaluation techniques can be used with the vast majority of the students, they are not suited to the natural discoverer. Johnny Jones works like a beaver, slaves over his homework and gets an A. Tommy Smith also gets an A, but it was completely effortless to him. Isn't there a weakness in evaluation here?

As a possible solution we offer these three alternative methods of evaluation which we have seen work well for the natural discoverer:

THE CONTRACT EVALUATION FORM—Figure 12-1 shows a contract evaluation form. This is given to the natural discoverer who may be working either within or outside the class, to fill out. Notice that it makes him reflect on what he has learned, pinpoint his own weaknesses, and while doing this, it is totally relevant to what the child has done and his own abilities. If a mark *must* be given according to your school's policy, it is now more equitably determined by the student and the teacher through the use of this form.

FIGURE 12-1

CONTRACT EVALUATION FORM

Your Name ——————— Contract Title ———————————

Date Approved ——————— Date Completed ———————————

Number of Weeks it Took and Why?———————————————

1. Where did you get the idea for the contract?

2. Did you plan well? Why or why not?

3. Did you enjoy this contract? Is there more to learn about this subject? Do you think you will ever return to it?

4. Did you encounter any problems in the contract? What were they? How were they solved or did you solve them?

5. Did you accomplish your objective? Why or why not?

6. Did you learn something new? about yourself? about others?

THE PROJECT EVALUATION FORM—The project evaluation form is seen in Figure 12-2. This is directly tied to the independent study method which we described earlier in the chapter.

THE ORAL AND/OR WRITTEN ESSAY EXAM FOR BULK MATERIAL—In essence this method has a child tell or write everything he knows about a particular area of study. He can be questioned on it, and he must be ready to defend any statements he makes. This method goes with the seminar method also described earlier.

Please understand, we are not advocating any of these methods over another, nor are we saying that grades or parent conferences are wrong. What we are saying is that for years the natural discoverer, the gifted or exceptional child, has been evaluated like everyone else in the system. This child, however, is *not* like everyone else—he knows it, the other students know it, and we know it, too.

Any method of evaluation that overlooks the *child* involved becomes less than human. If a grade on a report card is nothing more than the average and tally of figures on a sheet of paper, then perhaps we have taken the first step toward the horrifying future of cold, impersonal machines taking the place of teachers as depicted by some of our finest science fiction writers. A machine teaches history—we teach Johnny and Mary and Fred.

Take whatever method you choose to evaluate the natural discoverer, but make certain you leave the child in the evaluation. Though we are speaking here of the natural discoverer, make certain you apply this philosophy to all members of your class. They, too, deserve a fair, impartial, and above all relevant evaluation.

FIGURE 12-2

PROJECT EVALUATION FORM

Evaluator _____

Student _____

Date _____

Please check below each statement the word, phrase, or space which most closely corresponds with your evaluation. If none of the available comments apply, please write your own comments. If you are unable to judge an item, make no marks.

* *

   1. Interest level throughout the project
     ( ) consistently high ( ) improved ( ) sufficient
          ( ) dropped ( ) low

   2. Accepts responsiblity for:
     a. Attendance and punctuality
       ( ) dependable ( ) improved ( ) sufficient
          ( ) decreased ( ) undependable

    b. Maintaining project and room
      ( ) dependable ( ) improved ( ) sufficient
        ( ) decreased ( ) undependable

3. States in writing the goals of study (check what applies)
   ( ) challengingly ( ) originally ( ) realistically
      ( ) specifically ( ) measurably

4. Lists in writing the methods of doing study (check what
   applies)
   ( ) clearly ( ) realistically ( ) in logical order
      ( ) in ample detail ( ) vaguely

5. Locates pertinent information from a variety of sources
   ( ) most ably ( ) improved ( ) sufficient ( ) least ably

6. Organizes information and materials well
   ( ) consistently ( ) improved ( ) sufficiently
      ( ) decreased ( ) seldom

7. Organizes time wisely
   ( ) consistently ( ) improved ( ) sufficiently
      ( ) decreased ( ) seldom

8. Analyzes and criticizes (Such as: compares viewpoints,
   questions, judges, evaluates information, solves problems,
   uses logic, corrects errors, etc.)
   ( ) consistently ( ) improved ( ) sufficiently
      ( ) decreased ( ) seldom

9. Creates; produces original product; thinks original
   thoughts
   ( ) consistently ( ) improved ( ) sufficiently ( ) seldom

10. Work with little or no supervision
   ( ) consistently ( ) improved ( ) sufficiently
      ( ) decreased ( ) seldom

11. Amount of teacher guidance needed as project progressed
   ( ) less and less ( ) same as when started ( ) more and more

12. Makes a final presentation which is (check what applies)
   ( ) interesting ( ) creative ( ) well organized

13. Demonstrates increased general knowledge of study
( ) most increase ( ) moderate increase ( ) little increase

14. Demonstrates increased depth of understanding (Example: Learning specialized vocabulary and adding own opinions)
( ) most increase ( ) moderate increase ( ) little increase

15. Submits a written bibliography of sources utilized (Check any that apply)
( ) complete ( ) in proper form ( ) incomplete ( ) none

16. Shares results with other students and teachers
( ) most ( ) high moderate ( ) low moderate ( ) least

17. Submits, throughout the project, evidence and evaluation of work done.
( ) consistently ( ) regularly ( ) improved
( ) sufficiently ( ) irregularly

18. Demonstrates ability to evaluate how well the above objectives were accomplished
( ) very accurately ( ) improved
( ) sufficiently ( ) poorly

19. Looks into suggestions which are offered
( ) consistently ( ) sometimes ( ) seldom

20. In making decisions about the project, the advisor gave
( ) too much help ( ) sufficient help ( ) too little help

21. More decisions about my own work were made in
( ) independent study ( ) regular class

22. Regular class work has
( ) improved ( ) remained high ( ) remained low ( ) gone down

23. Followed through to completion
( ) no pushing ( ) some pushing ( ) very much pushing

I would evaluate this project as: ACCEPTABLE _____
                                     UNACCEPTABLE _____

On a separate sheet of paper, list any strengths and/or weaknesses of the project itself, any evaluation of goals and methods accomplished, or other comments.

COMMENTS

Chapter 13

How to Effectively
Evaluate
Your Discovery Techniques

Don't get turned off by the title of this chapter. "Evaluation," to most teachers, conjures up images of stacks of test papers, endless hours of marking and grading, and tiresome record keeping. That is not what we have in mind. What we will be doing in this chapter is offering you a roadmap which allows you to chart your successes in order that you may get there again and again and again.

THE "HOWS AND WHYS"
OF EVALUATING SUCCESS

What is your criteria for evaluating the success or failure not only of the discovery techniques in this book, but of any educational technique? Really, it is very simple. If it worked for you—it succeeded; if it failed—it didn't. That may sound simplistic, but isn't it the case?

But be warned, just because that dynamic technique we tried this year was so successful, doesn't mean that we can whip it out next year and expect it to have the exact same results. Why not? If it's a good technique it will work all the time, right? Wrong. A given technique may have worked for us under one particular set of circumstances. It may not be relevant, however, under an alternate set of circumstances.

We can hear you saying, "Are they telling us that all the techniques we've read so far can only be used once!" Not at all!

What we are saying is that along with those techniques we gave you methods of evaluating them.

Throughout the book we have tried to help you pinpoint the situations, needs, and goals of *your* classroom. We had you fill out the Discovery Potential Guide which actually had you evaluate all the assets and needs for your given circumstances. Next, there was the Personal Preference Chart. A brief review of it after several months allows it to become an evaluative tool, for it will tell you if you have been accomplishing your goals. We showed you techniques for charting both the social and skill development of your students. Again, a review of these charts will show you if you are succeeding. We have further explained such items as a method for determining patterns in disruptions, the teacher's project guide, and how to project the best avenues of success for underachievers. These forms, taken as a whole, present a better picture of your class within a given time span and within a specified unit of work than any diagnostic tests we have seen. They will not only tell you where you were, but how far you have come.

If, after reviewing these forms, you have determined that you have succeeded with your class, they will also allow you to plan the guidelines that will take you there next year. Through their study you will not only be able to tell what techniques have worked, but under what circumstances they have worked. Armed with this knowledge you will be able to select the proper type of technique when a particular set of circumstances arise again.

PRACTICAL TECHNIQUES
FOR RECORD KEEPING

Remember back in Chapter III when we asked you to start a looseleaf notebook? Do you also remember how we asked you to add to it every now and then? We do hope you didn't think we were being facetious. We had very practical aims in mind. Let us take the time now to show you what that notebook will look like and what it will do for you.

We hope your notebook was a sturdy ring-type binder, for it will get a lot of use. The purchase of plastic page covers should prove valuable and a set of tabs will stand you in good stead. Assuming that you have or can get these stationery supplies, let us take you through the notebook and show you what it should look like.

In the very beginning of the book is the Discovery Potential Guide, followed by the Personal Preference Chart and Diagram. Next comes the series of Skill Charts and Social Diagrams that have been done over the year. Following that there will be the chart work you have done on various underachievers, projects, etc. This is all work that you have done relative to the particular class you have this year. Consequently, at the conclusion of the year, *this material will be discarded.* In order to remain valid to the class you have *now,* new charts must be drawn up with each succeeding class. If you wish, a synopsis of several paragraphs may be drawn up. This may be valuable if you have learned something about your teaching over the period of a year (Skill work, for example, was better taught in the mornings.). Just make sure you don't hold your next year's class to the same standards.

The remainder of the notebook is divided into sections which have such headings as Skill Work, Projects, Language Arts, Science, Underachievers, etc. *This is material that will be kept from year to year.* These are the techniques that you have successfully used under each heading, their evaluations, and your comments on their use and effectiveness. These will provide the basic stockpile for next year's Discovery Notebook. There is only one thing that we have mentioned in all of this that we haven't shown you yet, and that is the Guide for Evaluating Discovery Techniques. This Guide will be of tremendous help to you in determining the potential future success of those techniques you have found to be successful this year.

HOW TO DETERMINE
WHAT TECHNIQUES TO RE-USE

Remember that the second part of our premise for this book was that once we had shown you a way to success, we would show you how to get there again and again. The Guide For

Evaluating Discovery Techniques will be your greatest asset toward fulfilling that promise.

For each technique that you used, there was a specific reason why you used it. There was a special set of circumstances and a special problem you wanted to solve. Because that situation may never come up in *exactly* the same way again, you should know how to adapt basically good techniques to more than one situation and more than one set of circumstances. With that in mind, let us take a look at the Guide.

If you look at Figure 13-1, you will notice that the top of the Guide uses material gathered from the Discovery Potential Guide. The next section is Execution Information—time and materials needed and basic requirements. The next section is the vital one—Situational Data. This is the situation that existed that made you choose this technique. Please note, this is *not* a description of the technique, but rather a description of the *situation* that called for the technique. Finally, there is the section marked Evaluative Comments. The first questions under this section deal with what you thought were the assets or faults of the technique *at the time you tried it.* The final question deals with the adaptation you thought of, *at the time,* for any future use of the technique.

FIGURE 13-1

GUIDE FOR EVALUATING
DISCOVERY TECHNIQUES

Teacher's Name_____ Date Used _____

Discovery Potential Guide Data

Age/Grade Level _____ Grouping _____
                  (K-8)   (Homogeneous, Hetero-
                                  geneous, Continuous
                                  Progress)

                              Level _____
                                   (A, B, C, D, F, Remedial)

Number of students present___ Number of students involved___

Basic Activity _____

_____

_____

Execution Information

Materials needed for preparation _____

_____

_____

Materials needed for execution _____

_____

_____

Time needed for preparation _____Explain_____

_____

_____

Time needed for execution _____

Situational Data

     Tell your reason(s) for using this particular technique. Use no names, but be specific.

_____

_____

_____

_____

EVALUATIVE COMMENTS

1. How well did this technique work? Explain.

_____

_____

_____

_____

2. What could you have done to make it even more effective? Explain.

_____

_____

_____

3. How could you adapt this technique? Give situation and subject.

_____

_____

_____

_____

Additional Comments.

_____

_____

_____

_____

In your notebook, you would place the Guide evaluating a given Discovery Technique inside the plastic cover containing the technique you used. By the end of the year, you will have pages, some thick and some thin, that all look approximately the same as you leaf through your notebook. These are invaluable references you will use again and again.

Since we want to keep this whole thing practical, we must do something to trigger our memories and help in the adaption process. We have come up with one that works for us, and hopefully it will work for you as well. To your stationery supplies add one box of silver stars, one box of gold stars, and a couple of boxes of signal dots in various colors. If the technique was O.K.; that is, moderately successful but nothing spectacular, you might give it a silver star. If, on the other hand, it was a bullseye, dead-center, fantastically successful and enjoyable for you and the class, then give it a gold star. If the technique falls into neither of the above categories, *don't throw it out.* Leave it blank, for it just might earn one next year.

When you go through your notebook, you will be able to categorize your techniques by using the colored signal dots. To each category, assign one of these dots. In this way, you will be able to tell at a glance into which category a technique falls simply by its color. The basic categories are:

RED—one situation/one subject
BLUE—one situation/multiple subjects
GREEN—social situation
YELLOW—project situation
ORANGE—underachiever situation
BROWN—natural discoverer situation

It should be clear to you that several of the categories can fit under others as well. For example, when working with an underachiever, you might have used a technique for one situation/one subject. You guessed it—that technique gets one orange *and* one red dot. Now a picture should be forming, because all your techniques *won't* look alike.

When preparing for next year's class, correlate the techniques in the latter part of your notebook under various categories. (You could use page tabs.) Again, the first part of your notebook will hold the charts and diagrams you will prepare with your new class in mind. The middle section (divided into

subjects as it was this year) is blank, awaiting the new techniques *you* will discover during the coming year. Some of the
techniques that will go in that middle section will come from
that resource section of "winners" you built this year. You can
re-use those techniques completely assured of your success. A
couple of years of building, and you will find your Discovery
Notebook becoming as indispensable as your plan book or grade
book.

We do, however, give you a few words of caution. You
noticed that, when speaking of evaluating and adapting your
discovery techniques, we stressed that the most practical advice
we could offer on any technique of record keeping was never to
leave *anything* to memory. We can just hear you saying, "But I
have a fantastic memory!" We are sure you do, but please tell us
what you did the second week of September for Mary Beth;
remember, she's the one who kept reading "bad" for "bald"
and "pear" for "pearl"? See what we mean? Some techniques
are used so quickly and perhaps not repeated for the rest of the
year, that they can easily be misplaced or forgotten. Don't let
these gems be lost. Put them in a safe, secure place where you
will have them when you need them—your Discovery Notebook. However, don't go taking out a safety deposit box. These
successful techniques must be available—not only to you, but to
your fellow educators, too.

SHARING IDEAS—DISCOVERY
THROUGH DISCUSSION

In most professions, there is a feeling of collective research.
The "Team Effort," if you will, that says, "We did it!" when a
breakthrough is announced. Why doesn't this hold true in
education? First, we *are* a profession, and there *is* a great deal
of research being done in the field. But, do we share it? During
the preliminary work on this book, we must have heard a
hundred statements like, "Oh, you don't want to put this in; it
isn't good enough!" or "This is just something I do with *my*
class; you want something better." Please understand, modesty
is fine—in its place, but it has no place in education if it leads to

the feeling that all the good ideas belong to somebody else or will be forthcoming from some great unknown expert.

This is a tremendously self-defeating attitude. Most of the best creative educational thoughts come from the classroom teacher. After all, *she* is the one who has to make them work; *he* is the one who has to teach the class what they have to know. Their judgment as to what is successful or not successful is the best example of clinical research available. The classroom teacher bows to no one when it comes to knowing what to do with a class. Consequently, we have to get rid of the idea that what we do individually is not good enough for our peers.

How do we reverse this self-defeating trend? We do it by *sharing* our ideas. We must share our successes and our objective evaluations of them, and we must offer positive suggestions for adaptation. Finally, we must offer constructive hints for overcoming any problems we may have encountered. We realize that some of you may feel that this calls for you to act like some kind of expert. Well, what's wrong with that? When you use a technique, you know more about its ramifications at that particular moment than anybody else. We're not telling you to show off—just share, because as others learn from you, you will learn from them. Let's look at three methods of sharing your discovery with others.

We have had you start a Discovery Notebook. Share this idea with others. Then, as their Discovery Notebooks grow, share pages. If you have a couple of gold star techniques, why should your fellow educator not benefit from them? You may have been searching for one spectacular technique to stop an "itchy" problem once and for all. You notice that your friend never has that problem. Find out why. The technique he uses might be just the one for which you have been looking. Copying may be wrong for the students, but it is not for the teacher seeking solutions to problems. This borrowing and lending of pages from your Discovery Notebooks will add more jewels to each of your collections.

Another idea is to start a central receiving file for Discovery Techniques. This could be a large notebook kept in the library or a series of filed material kept in the Teacher's Room. When something happens that will be of benefit to anyone else—contribute it. Before starting anything new, check the file. Someone may have come up with an idea that, with your adaptation and creativity, could really turn your class on. In this type file, *nothing* is extraneous. A great technique that the kindergarten teacher used *can* be adapted to an eighth grade science class. All that is needed is the kindergarten teacher's evaluative comments, a particular need collectively shared, and the science teacher's creativity and ingenuity.

This central Discovery Notebook should be compiled using record keeping symbols which are readily understood by everyone. You may or may not use the system that we gave you, but whatever method you choose, keep it consistent. We would further suggest that all contributions be placed in plastic page covers for durability.

One other idea that has been used with great success is grade level and/or subject discovery meetings. Call it "rapping," call it "brainstorming," call it whatever you please, but sitting down together on a regular basis and sharing and critiquing Discovery Techniques of yours and others will have a twofold benefit. First, it will keep you informed as to what others are doing, and secondly, you will begin to have the feeling that you are a working part of a cohesive unit. It doesn't matter if you do it in the teacher's room, at someone's home over a cup of coffee, or even in a local bistro if you are so inclined, but *share* those precious ideas!

DEVELOPING A DISCOVERY LIBRARY

There are four major methods you can use to develop your Discovery Library:

BECOME A PAPER CUTTER—Remember that article you saw in that magazine last month? Wasn't that fantastic insight into the way a child's mind works? Would you like to be able to use it and share it? *Cut it out!* Whenever you come across a picture, an idea that you can turn into a Discovery Technique, a poem, or a story that will help you in your classroom or even help you in expanding your educational philosophies, keep it to ponder, postulate, and practice.

BECOME A READER—This seems obvious; you're reading this book, aren't you? That's fine, but we are speaking of reading other things as well. Read at least two of the books that your *students* will be reading. Keep these in your Discovery Library and re-read them periodically, for they will make you aware of the type of material with which your students must deal. When you are finished reading the book, review it in capsule form (a paragraph will do), and you will have a point of reference for assigning books to students.

BECOME A COLLECTOR—Start now to collect any and all materials that can be *practically* used by you or your class to inspire discovery. Notice that we have stressed "practically," for we do not want you to become pack rats. However, you will meet with a variety of materials which your classes can *really* use. How about those games in that magazine or those shiny stones that first graders love to use for counting or that box of sea shells that you got on your vacation? Could they be a lesson in social interaction, applied mathmatics, or a natural discoverer's science project? Just remember, keep only what is practical.

BECOME AN OBSERVER—There is nothing to stop you from observing other classes. You are a professional observing another professional, and you will both gain from the experience. It is good to have someone tell you about a technique, but it is better to observe it in action. Also, become aware of what the media is presenting to your students. Watch some of *their* TV shows and listen to some of *their* radio. Even in the daily operation of your school, train yourself to observe. Watch the playground, listen to the lunchroom, and feel the halls. All these are part of the child's *milieu*, and, as such, are instrumental in helping you form relevant discovery techniques.

"So," you are saying, "what do I do with all this stuff which you've decided I need?" Easy now, we've even got a place for it.

It's called your Discovery Library. The first part of your Discovery Library was your Discovery Notebook. The second item is a book which we'll name *Educational Resource Material.* This is a notebook much like the first one, except that this is the place you put those clippings and articles. Personally, we collect them all year long and read and categorize them in the summer. The third set of items are books that you have found particularly helpful—like the one you are now holding, hopefully. Also include that fantastic book on reading techniques for your age level, etc. Finally, *one* cardboard box. That's where you keep the sea shells! See why we said they had to be practical—you're only allowed one box, no cheating, now!

Now you have to find some place permanent to house your library. Actually, it doesn't matter where you keep it. Your only guidelines are that it must be accessible and permanent. It must be the one place you can go and lay your hands on exactly what you want when you want it. With the exception of the Discovery Notebook which should be kept at your desk in school, you can keep it anywhere.

Finally, let everyone know that you are keeping a Discovery Library and suggest that they do the same. In this way you will be taking the first step toward opening vital channels of communication from which everyone will benefit—not the least of whom will be your students.

"PSSST! . . . PASS IT ON . . . "

What follows is a checklist. We'd like you to mentally check off the items that apply:

1. Did you gain any new insights into your classes or your school from the Discovery Potential Guide?
2. Did you pick up a new technique this year for handling social pressures in your classroom?
3. Did you learn or come up with any new ideas about seating or room arrangements?
4. Did the use of empathy or techniques like "The Actor" help you to handle an itch?
5. Did you come up with any new teaching techniques after reviewing the Skill Chart?

6. Did your class enjoy "The Spangled Pandemonium?"
7. Did you find a way to make a subject "come alive?"
8. Did the production of homework in your class pick up because of any particular technique?
9. Did you get a new perspective on projects?
10. Did you find a new way of pinpointing an under-achiever's problems?
11. Did you find a new way to expand the horizons of your natural discoverer?
12. Did you find a way to capitalize on past success?

Did you?

YOU DID!

Well . . .

Psst! . . . Pass it on!

Chapter 14

Teachers, Students, Parents, and Us— A Timely, Relevant Dialogue

---

Over the years we have been involved in innumerable discussions with parents, teachers, students and administrators. Whether it has been in a formal meeting, panel discussion, in-service training session, or just while "rapping" on education, many provocative questions have arisen which have required straight-forward and honest answers. We have taken a number of them and placed them in this chapter along with our answers. These questions are the ones which we feel are particularly pertinent to the many avenues of discovery. Some of them deal specifically with this book. We hope that if a similar question has crossed your mind, you will find that question answered here.

For the purposes of clarification, we have indicated at the end of each question whether it was asked by a teacher, student, parent, or administrator. Remember that any question is valid if the person who asks it is honestly seeking an answer.

You seem to think that teachers have a lot more say in school policy than they do in my school. How would you expect me, for instance, to set up a program for the gifted or exceptional child where he could come and go as he needed? I couldn't get away with that in my school! (Teacher)

You are correct in inferring that administrators set school policy, but you are less than correct in assuming that the policy is arbitrary and unchangable. We have met very few administrators who will not listen to an idea *if* (and it's a big *if*) it is carefully thought out. This means time required, funds needed, and the methodology for practical implementation. All this must be done *before* you propose it. In order for any new program to be adopted, the person in charge must get the feeling that one, it has a reasonable chance of working; two, you are committed to it; and three, it is possible to do it under the given school's circumstances. After all, a school that has just had to drop its lunch program due to lack of funds is not going to spring for twenty-five tape recorders and a hundred microscopes. They just can't. If you keep these things in mind, then we honestly feel that you could do it in your school with your administrator.

You place great emphasis on the teacher's interaction with students. What do you conceive of as the parents role in the discovery process? (Parent)

The parent's role in the discovery process or anything else to do with their child, for that matter, is tremendously important. Too many parents and teachers conceive of education as a twelve year war fought over the body and mind of the child. "What are they doing to my baby?" screams the parent; "What must those parents be doing at home?" screams the teacher. In the meantime, the child is in the middle and gains nothing. In fact, he loses his chance at having the two greatest forces in his life working together for his benefit. Isn't it the goal of the home and the school to prepare the child for his future? This can only be accomplished if the home and the school work *together.* Discovery happens on both sides of the school door. Since a Discovery Technique of its very nature works for and within the child, what does it matter if the child discovers in the classroom of his school or in that other classroom called his home?

I think the way schools are set up is dumb! They tell ya something in class, spend two weeks on it, get ya all interested in it, and then ya don't meet it again until it's "reviewed" next year! What happens if I want to know more about something right now? Why do they do that? (Student)

First of all, the reason they do it is because schools are like a smorgasbord. You know what that is, right? You do. Good. You get a little bit of this and a little bit of that. Sometimes you like what you put on your plate, and sometimes you don't. But you don't know until you've tried a little bit of everything. The nice thing about a smorgasbord, though, is that if you find something you really like, you can go back again and again and get as much of it as you want. But, no waiter is there to serve you; you have to go get it yourself. That's what happens in your class. Your books and your teacher introduce you to a little of this and a little of that, and, if it's important, they do it a couple of times. If you find something you really think is great, go back for more. Go to your teacher and tell her. Like a smorgasbord, she won't serve it up to you on a platter, but she'll sure tell you where you can go to get more. Make up your own menu.

You seem to expect a great deal of time to be spent outside of class by your teachers. Where do you find such dedicated people? (Teacher)

According to that clock on the wall it is now 8:26. Why aren't you home watching television? You already have the answer to your question in the answer to our question. You're here because you want to learn and share ideas. By a fast count, there're maybe thirty-five others here in that same category. Where do we find such dedicated people? Don't look now, friend, but you are one.

You talk about the fact that values don't change but lifestyles do. How much of the instilling of values is the school's responsibility? (Parent)

Schools got into trouble when they tried to control lifestyles. Remember, a lifestyle is nothing more than social expression—a fad if you will. If you don't think lifestyles change, just look at an early album cover of the Beatles and remember the furor about those "long-haired weirdos" from England. Today, we can only wish that our sons would look as neat and well groomed. That is a lifestyle. And, frankly, the school has no business there.

On the other hand, values are passed on within the fiber of

our society from one generation to the next. That "honesty is the best policy" was true when it was written hundreds of years ago, and it still stands true today. If a teacher were to teach that in her classroom, she is merely reinforcing socially acceptable norms. No parents in the world want their child to be dishonest, lazy, a thief, or petty. In fact, you spend a great deal of time and effort trying to instill wholesome qualities in your child. Would you not expect the school to reinforce your training? Yes, the schools do have a responsibility here—to you, certainly, and to your child as well.

You seem to assume that kids come in eager and ready to learn and never cause problems. Doesn't this smack of starry-eyed idealism? (Teacher)

On the surface—perhaps, but we have never mentioned a technique that you could not practically implement in the worst class you have—and we can defend that statement. We have given you techniques for handling behavioral problems *within the classroom;* techniques for handling the underachiever *within the classroom;* and techniques for handling the turned off, bored, natural discoverer *within the classroom.* We have seen them work, we have kept them practical and relevant, and we have always kept the classroom teacher in mind. Certainly not all children come to you bright eyed and bushy tailed. Certainly, some children are definite pains. Certainly, you will have problems from now until they toast you at your retirement dinner. None of us have grown old by looking at kids through rose-colored glasses. But kids, most kids, can be reached. We have tried to give you the practical tools *you* can *use.*

Do you feel that discovery techniques are relevant in today's education? I mean, in terms of individualization and motivation and the changing nature of today's society? And are you basing any of your techniques on the ramifications of the "thorough and efficient" court rulings? And do you feel that teachers will respond positively to these techniques and use them in their classrooms? And do you feel you are making a valuable contribution to educational research? (Teacher)

Yes.

*Teachers in school literally drown in paper. We have to send out
notices and forms and bulletins on a daily basis. Granting that
your charts and diagrams are valid and necessary to your
program, aren't you compounding the paper problem?* (Administrator)

In the beginning, yes. The first time a teacher fills out a
Discovery Potential Guide, it will take him some time. Moreover, when all the charts and forms are completed there will be
quite a bit of paper. The criteria to be considered, however, is
will this time be well spent—that is, will it make your teacher's
classroom time, plans, and activities more effective, more
relevant, more interesting, and more certain of success. We feel
it will. Also, as they become more familiar with the material
and begin building that stockpile we were speaking of, the
actual time spent will decrease. Moreover, those bulletins and
notices that you were speaking of are of their very nature
transient. They come out each day, are read and noted, and
then discarded to be replaced by the next day's notice. We,
however, are referring to forms that the teacher completes *once,*
and then *uses* all year long. Even the forms that have to be
updated periodically are checklists that don't require all the
time in the world to do.

*Each day my child comes home and tells me he is bored,
doesn't learn anything, and doesn't want to go back to school.
Aside from telling him that he just has to put up with it for the
next nine years, how do you think I should approach his
problem?* (Parent)

Please understand that because we don't know you or your
child it is impossible to give a specific answer. The best
suggestion we can make is that you get together with your
child's teacher and the school's guidance facilities and talk out
the problem. However, you might consider these three avenues.
First, your child may have encountered a physical problem that
makes him want to stay out of school. You know, a bully on
the playground, a group of children who tease him, or, horror
of horrors, a girl who is "in love" with him. Another possibility
is that he may be at either end of the educational spectrum. His
"boredom" may actually be frustration because the work is too
difficult for him, or he may actually be bored because the work

is too easy. Finally, he may have hit a snag in a particular subject or activity that will work itself out in time. In any case, go see his teacher and guidance counsellor as soon as possible, and you'll be able to work it out—together.

The trend in education seems to be toward individualization, yet you seem to be placing a great deal of emphasis on group and class work. Why? (Teacher)

Because nobody lives in an isolated cabin on top of a mountain. No one works in a vacuum, lives in a vacuum, or exists in a vacuum. We are all part of a society, and we all interact. Children must learn how to relate to other people. We don't mean just the social niceties, but we are talking about collectively learning and sharing new ideas, new skills, and new perspectives. That combination makes for progress of the individual as well as the group. In our techniques, we spend a great deal of time on the individual, but only as he must relate to those around him. We feel that this type of interaction is of ultimate benefit to the individual child.

Whether you call it contractual learning, continuous progress, open classroom, or an independent study program, the point to remember is that *it is not for everybody.* Some children work extremely well and achieve fantastic results within these setups. It works for them, they obviously like it, and it is succeeding— for them. However, so much depends upon the maturity of the child, his level of self-discipline, his relationship to the personality of the coordinating teacher, and the availability and relevancy of material, that for some children it just does not work. Some children can not put pressure upon themselves; others put too much. Some children need the structure, direction, and support that they can only receive in a traditional classroom. If a basic premise of individualization is that no one thing works for all students, we agree. And that includes individualization.

By all means try it with your classes, but please note we said *try.* If you have the kind of class in which it works, then fine—use it. If it doesn't work, stop the experiment. Don't consider it a failure. Don't blame the class, yourself, or the technique. It is just that in that particular situation, it did not work. Find something that does.

*How come some teachers don't seem to like kids, while others
act like they really do?* (Student)

We think that's an honest question, and we're going to try to
answer it honestly. This is how we see it. Sometimes people get
so tied up with problems that they can't seem to see anything
else. Especially when you're a teacher, your problems are big
and noisy and your successes are quiet. How many times have
you heard a kid say to a teacher, "Boy, that was great!"
compared to, "Yechhh! Do we gotta do that boring junk again?"
The problems keep happening, and they happen right now,
every day. Whatever successes there are usually come in the
future and sometimes you're lucky if you see them at all. One
day a young man came up to us on the street and told us that
he was graduating college and was going to be a biologist. He
said that this was because when he was in eighth grade, one of
us had taught a class that had so inspired him, he had never lost
the interest and enthusiasm that made him go on and learn
more. That really made us feel good, but we would never have
known that if we hadn't met him by accident. Each day, however, we can see the fights and stealing and lying. If you're
not careful, this can begin to get to you after a while. It's not
that some teachers don't like kids, it's just that some of them
may have lost their perspective. The ones whom you say still
seem to like kids are the ones who are still getting a kick out of
the quiet successes. The next time that you do something in
class that you like, really like, don't keep it to yourself. Go tell
your teacher that you liked it.

*You place great emphasis on child-generated discovery. How is a
teacher to know what is a genuine question which the child has
thought out, and what is a question purely intended to
sidetrack me or the class so they won't have to continue with
what they've been doing?* (Teacher)

That's some question, especially since we were both very
good at sidetracking when we were students. What we do
remember from our own experience, however, is that we were
never really interested in what we brought up. We just asked the
question, as you said, to keep the class from going on with the
particular lesson. If the teacher would have given us a brief

answer and then told us to look up some more information to
report to the class before we continued on, it would have
stopped right there. If we were serious about the question,
however, we would have looked it up, reported back, and gone
on to discover even more about it. We would think that this is
your key. The question might be irrelevant, or it might be real,
and we can none of us afford to establish a classroom environment where a child is afraid to ask a question. If, however,
when a child asks a question, it is answered briefly and to the
point by someone who appears interested, then you can go on
to point out where he can find more about it and ask if he
would care to research it and report to the class about it. You
may find that if the question was of the sidetracking nature it
will end there for the child will not want to go on and do the
work, but you have still positively reinforced his understanding
and that of the class that you are willing to accept questions. If
the question was a serious one, then he will do the work, and
who knows, that may inspire the entire class's discovery in a
particular subject area.

*You touched on an area with which I am familiar. You spoke of
relevance of reading material. I have found that to be a real
problem. For instance, some books have the children read about
farm life, and most of my students have never seen a cow
except on television. Do you have any suggestions on how I can
make their reading material relevant not only to their grade
level abilities but to their own lives?* (Teacher)

You have several avenues of approach to this problem. You
can either bring the books to the kids or the kids to the books.
If you feel that their books contain material which, while not
relevant to their lifestyle now, may be relevant sometime in
their future, then perhaps a well planned, carefully thought out
and previewed, and well-executed field trip, to that farm, for
example, may prove beneficial and give them something to
which they *can* relate. If you can't take field trips, a parallel
film strip, movie, or outside speaker may do just as well.

You may feel however, that the material must be relevant to
them *now*. If that is the case, go see your reading supervisor and
explain your situation. She may be able to help you. If you

don't have such a person, write to various publishers describing your class and their background. Be sure to include their age, reading level, and anything else you would consider relevant. You may find that the particular publisher has a series geared to just your type of class. In some cases they will send you samples; in other cases they send you reading lists, but they are more than anxious to help. From this you may be able to requisition books that will be meaningful to your class in your particular set of circumstances.

Since reading is the first step toward discovery, we agree with you that relevant material is important, especially on the lower elementary level. Keep them reading!

Do ya have to learn all the time? Can't ya just have fun?
(This question, asked by a third grade student, led to the following dialogue.)

Do you like games?
Uh-huh.
So do we. What's your favorite game?
Checkers.
That's a good game. Who taught you how to play?
My daddy.
You mean, there was a time you didn't know how to play checkers, and somebody, your Daddy, had to show you how?
Sure, ya gotta know how to jump and make kings and everything like that.
So, you had to learn it, right? But now you're having fun?
Yeah.
Well, that's the way it is with a lot of things: you gotta learn about them before you can have fun with them. Besides, didn't you have fun with your Daddy when he was showing you how to play checkers?
Yeah.
Sometimes things can be hard to learn, and you really have to work at it. But, think about it, if you never learned how to count, how would you know how much money you had to save to get your Daddy a birthday present? Your Daddy likes birthday presents, doesn't he?
He sure does.

See, learning and fun can go together.

How do you see the administrator's role in this discovery process you talk about? (Administrator)

The administrator's role in the discovery process is not only important; it's vital. It is no secret that the administrator sets the tenor of the building, the morale of the learning environment, call it what you will. If the administrator is genuinely interested in the educational growth of his students, dynamically and actively involved in that growth, and, and this we must stress, open and responsive to relevant suggestions which will sponsor and continue that growth, you can't help but have a discovery oriented school. The parents will have a school that is responsive to the needs of their children, the faculty will be working in a professional atmosphere that engenders professional growth and development, and the students will have a school that is both interested in them and interesting to be in. As an administrator make sure that faculty meeting time becomes a two-way street for communication; be certain that you go into classrooms, not as an evaluator as much as an interested observer; talk to your students and let them know that you are interested in them. Then, this fine discovery-oriented place of growth and learning won't be a dream; it will be a reality—called *your school.*

I'm just one teacher—what can I do? (Teacher)

What can you do? Everything that you have to do, that's what. There is an old saying, and we don't know who said it, that goes, "Stand up and be counted or be counted among the missing!" You, with the exception of the parents, are the one who is *the most actively involved with the child's intellectual growth.* If you do not strive to make that child's school years as productive as possible, no one else will. For any given year, *you* are education to that child. Years later that child will look back upon that year as being either relevant, meaningful, and good, or irrelevant, non-productive, and a waste of time. You are the one who will determine his views.

Henry Adams said, "A teacher affects eternity; he can never tell where his influence stops." Without getting poetic, there could be a future doctor, statesman, mathematician, or social reformer sitting in your class right now. Isn't he worth your effort? If your stand on prejudice got rid of stereotyped thinking in one child, then he won't pass it on and the world will be that much better for it.

One teacher, dedicated, resolved, and vocal, can change the thinking of an entire faculty, can help change an entire school for the better. It can't be done by a screaming fanatic, but it can be done by a dedicated professional with a plan and purpose. Be that dedicated professional, have that plan, and you will achieve your purpose. Let it begin with you!

Index